# MASSILLON MEMORIES

## *The Inside Story of the Greatest Show in High School Football*

SCOTT H. SHOOK

*With a Foreword by*
***Earle Bruce***
*former Ohio State Head Coach*

 For information, address Massillon Memories Publishing Company, 1507 Wales Road N.E., Massillon, OH 44646. You may contact The Massillon Memories web site at HTTP://WEBMAIL.NETSCAPE.COM or via e-mail at MEMBERS.TRIPOD.COM/~MASSILLON TIGERS

ISBN 0-966 7027-1-9

*To Ruth Shook, my mother,*
*for her love and confidence*
*in me to get the job done.*

*To Harry Shook, my father,*
*whose lifetime of stories about*
*the Massillon Tigers*
*were both inspirational*
*and accurate.*

# Acknowledgment

I have not attempted to cite in the text all the authorities and sources consulted in the preparation of this book. To do so would require more space than is available. This list would include many newspapers, magazines, libraries and many individuals.

The people of Massillon lived up to their reputation for cooperation. The Massillon Chamber of Commerce, who allowed me to scour their archives of Massillon Tigers history—then allowed me to use their copy machine—greatly aided my research. I also thank Bob Rohrer, Massillon Washington High School Principal, who gave me permission to use the photographs from the school's yearbooks, which make up most of the photographs in this book.

A big thanks goes to Gene Boerner, Bruce Campbell, Herb Campbell, Laurie Campbell, Jami Clevenger, Greg Cheek, Rick Connelly, Judy Crone, Becky Gatsios, Nancy Halter, Leanne Hope, Sue Repp, Dave Rossiter, Jim Rossiter, Randy Thorne, George Vellios, James Vellios, Douglas Waitley and Michelle Wolfe.

In the beginning, when the Great Creator was drawing plans for this world of ours, He decided there should be something for everyone. He gave us mountains that reach to the sky, deep blue seas, green forests, dry deserts, gorgeous flowers and gigantic trees.

Then he decided there should be football, and he gave us Massillon.

He created only one Massillon; He knew that would be enough.

Ron Maly
Des Moines Sunday Register
1978

## A Special Thanks

A man known warmly in Massillon as "Doc Immel" was *vital* in developing this book. Robert Immel, DDS, a former Massillon School Board President and Booster Club President, unselfishly shared interview tapes of Massillon football coaches he interviewed and who have since passed away. Without their stories, this book would be incomplete.

# Foreword

Massillon is a great football town. When you're born and raised in Massillon, Ohio, you are born to love the wonderful game of football and all the lessons that go with the game. Scott H. Shook was born and raised in Massillon and now is "paying back" to the game of football. His "Memories" bring the game as played and remembered in Massillon to a great new level.

Scott learned by writing sports since age 15 that by putting down new ideas or thoughts by coaches, players and boosters, you keep the magic of football going in Massillon. I like Scott's way of giving you some of the great moments in football, tradition, and everything else that *is* Massillon football.

Massillon was the greatest coaching experience I have ever had, *bar none.* They really approach the game in a big way. They care about winning, but they care more about their kids and the *experience.* Remember, football is King in Massillon—and I think Scott's book is a great tribute to Massillon and the great program they have had through the years.

## Earle Bruce

Head Coach, Ohio State 1979-1987
Head Coach, Massillon 1964-65

**Photographs, unless otherwise credited, courtesy of Washington High School, Massillon, Ohio.**

# Contents

Appendix

# Preface

It became important to me when I was seven years old. I was sent to my grandparents while my parents went to he Massillon/Upper Arlington game. It was bad enough that I didn't get to go. But going to bed without knowing the outcome of the game was almost too much.

My grandpa woke me early the next morning. "I've got bad news buddy, Massillon lost," he said, "but only by one point." I was crushed. I experienced the pain of a one point Massillon loss at a tender age.

I still feel a twinge of sadness when I remember that 7-6 loss. I guarantee you that *everyone* associated with that loss feels the same way, thirtysome years later. It cost Massillon the 1967 State Championship.

Massillon is a small steel town of 30,000. In its most glorious days, many of its players were tough sons of steel workers. Many of the big boys were bussed in from adjacent farmlands. The combination of tough city kids and rugged farmhands was successful. Massillon won 21 of its 22 state titles and *all* nine of its national titles between 1935 and 1970. When newspapers referred to Massillon, it was *Mighty Massillon.* Massillon believed they couldn't be beaten.

The Massillon Tiger Swing Band arrived on the scene in 1938 and thrilled audiences like no band ever had. With the addition of the band, the Massillon experience became known as The Greatest Show in High School Football.

With success came lofty expectations, national exposure and big crowds. The town grew to expect state championships. The players expected to win because their predecessors had won . It was their heritage. The unbridled success was contagious. The *average* attendance was often over 18,000 per game. A game against Cleveland Cathedral Latin drew 51,000 fans. The only football team in the state that outdrew Massillon was Ohio State.

Then the bottom fell out of the steel industry, and Massillon fell on hard times. Republic Steel, a leading employer, drastically downsized their operations. And the farmlands around Massillon grew to the point that they opened high schools of their own. Massillon's talent pool was shrinking.

But Massillon football has remained strong. Since 1932, Massillon has won 83 percent of their games. They remain a state power.

Ever since I started writing sports at age 15, I've dreamed of someday telling the nation about the Tigers. Through scores of interviews with players, coaches and sportswriters, and stacks of newspaper and magazine articles, I've attempted to capture the one-of-a-kind Massillon experience. I hope it moves you like it has moved me.

# Tradition

## MASSILLON TIGERS FOOTBALL TRADITION

In the 1920s, players were inspired by *Massillon Tigers Football Tradition*, harking back to the days of the professional Tigers, champions of 1903-07.

They were still talking about *Massillon Tigers Football Tradition* in the 1950s—thanks to **Paul Brown's** six straight state titles and the 52-game unbeaten streak that would have been 79 straight if not for an upset loss in 1937.

Players in the 1960s carried forth the *Massillon Tigers Football Tradition,* forged by the Phenomenal '50s and **Chuck Mather's** six straight state titles and 57-3 record. In the 1970s, players were touched by the *Massillon Tigers Football Tradition* through the glorious championships of **Leo Strang, Earle Bruce and Bob Commings**.

Today thousands of Massillon fans encircle Tiger Stadium, waiting in the cold rain for scarce tickets. The *Massillon Tigers Football Tradition* lives on...

**"Massillon's got that wonderful tradition, so from the day you're** born that's all you hear about. The great teams, the great players, the successes. You know the people in this town must really respect the young people—and they want to help them to do well. They've got something a lot of people are never going to be able to capture."

**Don James**

**Massillon Championship Quarterback, 1949**
**Record-breaking Quarterback,**
**University of Miami**
**National Championship Coach,**
**University of Washington, 1991**

*—on what makes Massillon, Massillon.*

**"Whenever people think of Massillon, to this day they think of football right away."**

**Paul E. Brown**

**Massillon Quarterback, 1923-25**
**Championship Coach: Massillon Tigers,**
**Ohio State Buckeyes and Cleveland Browns**
**Coach of 14 championship Teams**
**Founder of the Cincinnati Bengals**

*—on Massillon's identity as a football town.*

*Tiger Stadium, built in 1939.*
(Photo by Gallery Studio, Massillon, Ohio)

**"When you approach Massillon Stadium—and even before you** approach it, you see the flags waving downtown. And as you get near the stadium you see the searchlights going around. You hear the *calliope playing,* you hear the hawkers hawking, you see the Tiger in his cage. Then rockets go off at the Star Spangled Banner. And the Tiger roaring from the scoreboard. You know that something is happening. You get the *feel.*"

**Leo Strang**

**Massillon Championship Head Coach, 1958-63**
**State Champs, 1959-61, Nat'l Champs 1959, '61**
**Head Coach, Kent State University**

*—on how it feels to attend a Massillon game.*

## "Never waste a day."

**Don James**
**Massillon Championship Quarterback, 1949**
**Record-breaking Quarterback,**
**University of Miami**
**National Championship Coach,**
**University of Washington, 1991**

*—on a lesson he learned at Massillon that stayed with him throughout his coaching career.*

**"During the games us neighbor-hood kids were always playing** football in somebody's yard. We'd hear the bombs go off, see the fireworks go up in the air and we knew Massillon had scored a touchdown. On a regular basis they were shooting off bombs. We knew Massillon was winning."

**Tom Hannon**
**All-Ohio, 1972**
**Two-time All-Big 10, Michigan State, 1975-76**
**Minnesota Vikings Star, 1977-83**

*—on Massillon's tradition of announcing Tiger touchdowns to the town with fireworks.*

**“The signs in the windows, ‘A Massillon Tiger lives here.’ Fridays** in the junior high everybody wore Massillon Tiger jerseys. I just thought that was the greatest thing in the world. It was one city coming together for one common thing, one night a week. And that’s the most awesome thing in the world. I just thought, ‘How lucky am I to be a part of something like this? This is my heaven, my personal utopia.’ ”

**Chris Spielman**

**Massillon: 2-time All-Ohioan, All-American,**
**USA Today Defensive Player of the Year, 1983**
**Ohio State: 2-time All-American,**
**Lombardi Award Winner, 1987**
**NFL: Detroit Lions, Buffalo Bills, Since 1988**
**4 Pro Bowls**

*—on the Massillon feeling.*

**“Massillon has the best football tradition—no one’s even close to them, anywhere in the country.”**

**Gerry Faust**

**Head Coach, Cincinnati Moeller**
**Head Coach, Notre Dame**

*—on Massillon’s winning tradition.*

**"'My son, I want my son to be a football player.' This is something** he had lived for and dreamed about since he was a little boy. He got in the junior high, he came down as a sophomore, became a junior, and now he had his shot as a senior. If he was one of the ones who made it, he achieved one of the greatest things ever. You didn't have to worry about 'em. You didn't have to worry about their dedication to the game. Or to Massillon or to anything you wanted them to do."

**Tom Harp**

**Massillon Championship Head Coach, 1954-55**
**State Champs, 1954**
**Head Coach Duke, Cornell, Indiana State**
**Assistant to Colonel Blake at Army**

*—on Massillon Tiger players.*

**"In Massillon you win. You don't lose. You win. It's not a choice."**

**David Canary**

**All-Ohio, 1956**
**All-American, University of Cincinnati, 1959**
**4-Time Emmy Winner, "All My Children"**
**"Candy" on TV show "Bonanza"**

*—on Massillon's expectations.*

**"If I could handle the pressure at Massillon, I can handle the pressure here."**

**Earle Bruce**

**Massillon Championship Coach, 1964-65**
**State Champs, #2 in Nation, 1964-65**
**Head Coach, Ohio State University, 1979-87**

*—on whether he'd be able to handle the pressure of coaching at Ohio State University.*

**"The Massillon team was far, far, ahead of its time. The band was far,** far ahead of its time. And of course the stadium was, too. It was a most remarkable thing. This town of about 26,000 people was able to come up with a football team, a band, that held the entire interest of the town and it's never lost its grip. I've always been proud of the role my father played. And I think of all the things he did in his life, that's what pleased him most, I know that."

**Mike Brown**

**Coach Paul Brown's Son**
**General Manager, Cincinnati Bengals**

*—on his father's years in Massillon.*

**“There’s only one Massillon tradition. That’s why people come in from *Sports Illustrated and ESPN.***

It’s one of the great football traditions in the country. You go anywhere in the United States and mention you’re from Massillon, Ohio, and people say, ‘Oh, the Massillon Tigers.’ It’s a reputation that’s nationwide. The tradition is something different. It’s been there a long time. Not too many places in the United States have anything like it.”

**Mike Hershberger**

**Captain, All-Ohio, 1956**

**Major League Baseball Player, 1961-1971**

*—on the Massillon Tiger tradition.*

**“It didn’t take me long to see that if you wanted to be somebody in this town you had to play football, that’s what you had to do.”**

**Earl “Ick” Martin**

**Captain, All-Ohio Center**

**1939 State Championship Team**

*—on moving to Massillon from Canal Fulton.*

*Coach Tom Harp rides in the 1954 "Beat McKinley" parade.*

**"It was fantastic. The band was playing the "Tiger Rag" and "Carry** on for Massillon." All the students were there—and the enthusiasm for football. The way they reacted when I was introduced. I still get goosebumps even talking about it. I remember I said how happy I was to be there."

**Tom Harp**

**Massillon Championship Head Coach, 1954-55**
**State Champs, 1954**
**Head Coach Duke, Cornell, Indiana State**
**Assistant to Colonel Blake at Army**

*—on being introduced as Massillon's football coach.*

**"Massillon is one school that's been consistent. Traditionally a powerhouse down through the** years. They may have some down years, but not many. You can go back as long as you want to go back. That's one of the great high school programs in the nation. There were a lot of Massillon kids that I coached. A lot of 'em."

**Bo Schembechler**

**Legendary Michigan Head Coach**
**Ohio State Assistant Coach**

*—on Massillon.*

"***Tradition.*** **That's the one word that overshadows everything** here. I don't know where you'd find a high school football program with more tradition than we have here."

**Junie Studer**

**Massillon Tiger Sign Painter**
**Booster Club President, 1972**

*—on Massillon Tiger "Tradition."*

*Players prepare to burst through Junie Studer's hoop.*

**"It would be right before the game. He'd paint the hoops right there** on the scene. As a kid I remember him painting them in that garage next to the Massillon locker room. Later on he made them at the sign shop and the cheerleaders would pick them up and tape them together at the stadium. He's done that for over thirty years."

**Steve Studer**

**Massillon Center, 1970-71**
**All-American Center, Bowling Green, 1975**
**Massillon Strength Coach**

*—on watching his father, Junie Studer, paint the famous hoops that players run through before each game.*

**"In Massillon it was understood, you go the extra mile to do what** you can do to be successful on that football team. Extra training, extra work, extra effort. Not only my brothers told me that, but my mom and dad were saying, 'You've gotta do that.' "

**Jim Houston**

**Massillon: All-Ohio, 1955**
**Ohio State: All-American, 1958-59**
**Cleveland Browns: 4 Time Pro Bowl**

*—on the commitment expected from Massillon players.*

**"The older I got the more I came to appreciate what it was—it was really** a total package. The fans, the band, the cheerleaders. It wasn't just an isolated football team, it was part of a total package. There was a great camaraderie between the guys who were on the football team and the band."

**John McVay**

**All-Ohio Center, 1948**
**Head Coach, Memphis Southmen**
**Head Coach, New York Giants**
**Vice President and General Manager, San Francisco 49ers**

*—on the total entertainment package at Massillon.*

**"Every time we lost a game there was a 'For Sale' sign in the head coach's yard. *Every time.* If it** wasn't in the yard it was in the coach's garage because he'd moved it before we got there. I think it bothered all of them. That ceases to be funny. Because that's your livelihood. If I was the head coach and they did that to me I'd tell 'em right up front, if I see another one, you can take this job and shove it."

**Nick Vrotsos**

**Legendary Massillon Assistant, 1958-84**

*—on Massillon's anonymous tradition of planting a "For Sale" sign in the head coach's yard after a loss.*

*Scribes said it...*

**MASSILLON IS SMALL-SIZED COLUMBUS**

When the Tigers play football, Massillon makes believe it's the Fourth of July. Lincoln Way, the main drag of this northeast Ohio steel town, is gaily decorated with flags. Pictures of the young heroes adorn store windows. The Washington High Tigers have wrapped a 50-yard line around the town.

**HARRY GRAYSON, *AKRON BEACON JOURNAL*, 1950**

**"Any coach who has the talent is going to win in spite of himself—especially at Massillon. In a town** like Massillon, where you get the support like you get at Massillon, if you've got the kids, there aren't going to be many games you're going to lose. You have great facilities, great backing, great tradition—the town is crazy about football. I mean, how can you go wrong?"

**Nick Vrotsos**

**Legendary Massillon Assistant, 1958-84**

*—on the advantages of coaching at Massillon.*

**"At Massillon there's good 9-1's and there's bad 9-1's. Two of the** three 9-1 seasons were bad because we were 9-0 coming into the McKinley game and got beat. That's a bad 9-1 season. We were 9-1 one other time and that was a good season because we beat McKinley."

**Jack Rose**

**Massillon Head Coach, 1992-97**

*—on the importance of beating Canton McKinley.*

*Paul E. Brown*

*George "Red" Bird*

**"Paul and Dad were very much alike. They just expected a great deal. There were no excuses. You just did it."**

**Shirley Bird**

**Massillon Majorette, 1945**
**Band Director George "Red" Bird's Daughter**
**Cincinnati Bengals Entertainment Director**

*—on Paul Brown and her father, George "Red" Bird. Brown and Bird were neighbors in Massillon. Brown took Bird with him to Cleveland as the Browns' entertainment director. Bird also served as the Cincinnati Bengals' entertainment director, where Brown was owner and coach.*

**"The hospital provides the Booster Club with a list of the baby boys** born that month. One fella would paint on the footballs, 'Congratulations to a future Tiger.' The committee would deliver these footballs. These balls were sitting on mantels around the city. One of the proudest things for the parents was to get one of these for their baby son."

**Tom Harp**

**Massillon Championship Head Coach, 1954-55**
**State Champs, 1954**
**Head Coach Duke, Cornell, Indiana State**
**Assistant to Colonel Blake at Army**

*—on a proud Massillon tradition.*

**"The pressure to win is tremendous. And it's put on by yourself. When** you see the kids want to win the State Championship. The Booster Club and administration, they're all tremendously interested in how the program goes. So, the interest is the pressure."

**Earle Bruce**

**Massillon Championship Coach, 1964-65**
**State Champs, #2 in Nation, 1964-65**
**Head Coach, Ohio State University, 1979-87**

*—on the pressure to win at Massillon.*

*Massillon players take their first trip around the "blarney stone" in 1959.*

**"You were thrilled to play for the Tigers. You felt that you were the** best. You were disappointed if you didn't win. Because you worked at it. I've never worked harder in my life than as I did when we used to have to touch the blarney stone up on top of the hill. Everybody remembers the blarney stone. You beat the other teams not because you were better than them—you were better *prepared,* physically and mentally and fundamentally."

**Mike Hershberger**

**Captain, All-Ohio, 1956**

**Major League Baseball Player, 1961-71**

*—on Massillon's edge.*

**"Don't give up. We can always win. It didn't matter what the** circumstances were, how many points we were down, we could always do it. And you have to do it when you're out of breath and in the fourth quarter. That's the kind of thing that was instilled in us in Massillon—we can do it."

**Jim Houston**

**Massillon: All-Ohio, 1955**
**Ohio State: All-American, 1958-59**
**Cleveland Browns: 4 Time Pro Bowl**

*—on lessons he learned at Massillon that stuck with him throughout his career.*

**"Football—it's a trite saying—but it's a way of life here. People say,** 'Following high school football is a way of life?' Well, it is to a lot of people in this town. It's that one word: Tradition."

**Junie Studer**

**Massillon Tiger Sign Painter**
**Booster Club President, 1972**

*—on the importance of football in Massillon.*

*Earle Bruce*

**"I want to be remembered as a winning coach, that's** important in Massillon. I'm really proud of my record here. And I'm proud of the young men who played and of the assistant coaches. We were something that I believe in as far as football. We were a team."

**Earle Bruce**
**Massillon Championship Coach, 1964-65**
**State Champs, #2 in Nation, 1964-65**
**Head Coach, Ohio State University, 1979-1987**

*—on being remembered as a Massillon Coach.*

**TIGER TALES**

**SIX ELECTED CAPTAIN AT OHIO STATE**

Six Massillon players have been elected captain of Ohio State University's football team: Gordon Appleby (1944), Tommy James (1947), Jim Houston (1959), Bob Vogel (1962), David Whitfield (1969), Chris Spielman (1987). Only Tommy James, who opted to sign with the Detroit Lions, didn't serve his captaincy.

**"Leo Strang always said, 'Jack, enjoy it because you've just got to understand, it's never going to be good enough.' "**

**Jack Rose**

**Massillon Head Coach, 1992-97**

*—on fans' expectations of Massillon's coach.*

**"When I got the Massillon job I was getting phone calls from all over** the country. One was from Jack Mollenkopf. Jack said to me, 'Bob, do you understand that you took the toughest job in America?' I said, 'Ah, come on now Jack, *you're* at Purdue. Massillon isn't all that tough.' He said, 'Bob, in Massillon you are a football coach 365 days a year. You'll find out.' He was right."

**Bob Commings**

**Massillon Championship Coach, 1969-1973**
**State Champs, 1970**
**Head Coach, University of Iowa**

*—on advice from legendary Purdue coach Jack Mollenkopf.*

Bob Immel

**"We were like bellboys in a hotel. If you want** to know something that's going on in a hotel, ask the bellboy. They hear everything. And people talk in front of them thinking that you're going to ignore them. And they often say things in front of them that they don't realize might get out."

**Bob Immel**
**Student Manager, 1934-37**
**Booster Club President, 1956**
**School Board President, Team Dentist**

*—on the anonymity of the student manager.*

**"I've seen kids get hurt and just scream. They're not screaming** because they're hurt. They're screaming because they've worked so hard to get here and it's over. And they know it."

**Dale Walterhouse**
**Longtime Massillon Assistant**

*—on a Massillon player's desire to play.*

**"I had never seen such an attitude on a football team that they were going to win every football game. Every time they went out there."**

**Earle Bruce**

**Massillon Championship Coach, 1964-65**
**State Champs, #2 in Nation, 1964-65**
**Head Coach, Ohio State University, 1979-1987**

*—on Massillon's will to win.*

**"It's almost like a shock when you lose at Massillon. Like 'How could this ever happen?' "**

**Chris Spielman**

**Massillon: 2-time All-Ohioan, All-American,**
**USA Today Defensive Player of the Year, 1983**
**Ohio State: 2-time All-American,**
**Lombardi Award Winner, 1987**
**NFL: Detroit Lions, Buffalo Bills, Since 1988**
**Four Pro Bowls**

*—on losing at Massillon.*

**"I think I'm the keeper of the gate. I don't think you ever feel it's your** team. Because of the tradition, the things they've done here. You've got to kind of fit into that. There's a standard here that you have to meet. It's already developed. It's there. They know what they're doing. You've got to come in and do it that way. That's why they're successful. I think that's just a dynamic of any organization that's had the kind of success this one's had."

**Jack Rose**

**Massillon Head Coach, 1992-97**

*—on whether he felt Massillon was "his" team.*

**"I used to wake up in a cold sweat in the middle of the night during** the season. Start pacing, I couldn't sleep. So finally, I said, 'Nothing's worth this. I'm going to do the best I can, but I've gotta relax and enjoy the football.' So I had to change that a little bit. It's not the pressure, but the intensity."

**Earle Bruce**

**Championship Coach, 1964-65**
**State Champs, #2 in Nation, 1964-65**
**Head Coach, Ohio State University, 1979-87**

*—on the pressure to win at Massillon.*

**"When you lose, the fans can be very punishing. They come to** practice and sit in the stands and ask you why you lost. They come and watch you practice every day. Our stands are half full during practice. And you have to answer their questions about why you lost. Why didn't we do this, or why didn't we do that last week."

**Travis McGuire**

**All-Ohio Running Back, 1991**
**Stark County Player of the Year, 1991**
**Ohio Offensive Player of the Year, 1991**

*—on the scene at practice after a loss.*

**"That Tiger spirit is really what carried me through Ohio State and** Green Bay. Massillon set such a standard of excellence. When I went down to Ohio State I always made a point to be first in line for every drill. I was the last to leave the practice field. I learned a tremendous work ethic in Massillon."

**Steve Luke**

**All-Ohio, 1970**
**Three-time Rose Bowl Starter**
**Ohio State University, 1972-74**
**Green Bay Packers Captain**

*—on Massillon's influence on his football career.*

# The Pro Tigers

## THE BEGINNING

In 1903, professional football was born in Massillon, Ohio. And the seeds for the mighty Massillon Tigers family tree were planted in fertile soil.

This small Midwestern steel town came to life through its championship teams as they forged the early history of professional football.

The Tigers dominated early professional football, winning the sport's first five championships—their record, 41-2-1. They were undefeated at home through 1907.

Football legends **Jim Thorpe** and **Knute Rockne** battled six times between 1915 and 1917—Thorpe for Canton, Rockne for Massillon.

The fruits of Massillon's 22 Scholastic State Titles and nine Scholastic National Titles were sown from the success of their ancient ancestors—the mighty Massillon Pro Tigers.

**"There have been a few football games before. Yale has faced** Princeton. Harvard has tackled Penn and Michigan and Chicago have met in one or two steamy affairs. But these were not the real product when measured by the football standard set by the warring factions of Stark County Ohio, now posing in the pigskin lime-light."

**Grantland Rice**
**Legendary Sportswriter**

*—on the Massillon - Canton professional rivalry, 1906.*

**"Tonight Massillon is one seething mass of humanity. The** town is aflood with the light of many bonfires and burning tar barrels. Brass bands march through the streets, and the whole populace unites in celebrating the victory brought by the Tigers. From every window fly the orange and black streamers."

***Cleveland Plain Dealer,* 1906**

*—on one of Massillon's first downtown celebrations.*

# CANTON WHISTLES WERE NOT BLOWN

## *The Evening Independent*, 1905

*—on the Canton tradition of blowing factory whistles following football wins. This headline appeared after Massillon beat Canton 14-4 for the 1905 professional football championship.*

**"Little old Massillon was the happiest town in the country tonight. Red fire was burned for** hours. Men, women and children were on the streets, blowing horns and celebrating. The feeling here is that it was known all the time that the Tigers were best."

## *Cleveland Plain Dealer*, 1906

*—on Massillon's 13-6 Thanksgiving day win over Canton to claim the 1906 professional football championship.*

# The Fix Of '06

MASSILLON, NOV. 26—Manager **E.J. Stewart** of the Tiger football team and **H.A. Croxton**, one of the team's backers, charge that an attempt was made to bribe some of the Tiger players this season.

**Walter R. East** attempted to engineer the deal, with Canton Coach **Blondy Wallace** as an accomplice. They were backed by a crowd of gamblers who agreed to furnish $50,000 to be used for betting purposes and all expenses incurred, plus $5,000 in cash to the Tigers coach and management. But Massillon refused to be bought off.

Their scheme was for Canton to win the first game, Massillon to win the second game, with a third game in Cleveland to be played on its merits.

The proof of the reliability of this article, in the nature of the signed papers, can be found in the safe of the Massillon Iron and Steel plant. Mr. Croxton will be pleased to exhibit them to anyone.

## Newspaper Article, 1906

*—on a newspaper account of the "Fix of '06" that interrupted the Massillon-Canton professional rivalry for eight years.*

# Cradle of Coaches

## THE BEST PLACE TO COACH IN THE WORLD

*Paul E. Brown*

**MASSILLON** is a town of championship teams and championship coaches. **Paul Brown** (80-8-2) won six straight state titles (1935-40) and four national titles (1935-36, 1939-40) at Massillon. His creativity and success helped to make Massillon football the nationally famous total entertainment package it is today. **Chuck Mather's** tremendous success, 57-3, six straight state titles (1948-53) and three national titles (1950, 1952-53), ensured Massillon's winning tradition would endure. **Bud Houghton** (1941) and **Tom Harp** (1954) share the distinction of following legends—Brown and Mather. Both delivered state titles their first year

# Cradle of Coaches

*Chuck Mather*

as head coach—giving Massillon a *pair* of seven straight state title streaks (1935-41, 1948-54). Two coach **Stewarts** (no relation) were championship coaches at Massillon. **Ed Stewart** (24-1) dominated early professional football, leading the Pro Tigers to three titles (1903-05). **Dave Stewart** (38-9) won Massillon's first high school state title in 1922. **Elwood Kammer** (26-4) was a star running back for Massillon (All-Ohio, 1925). He coached Massillon to the 1943 state championship. **Sherburn Wightman** (17-1-1), led the Pro Tigers to two championships (1906-07). **Hap Fugate** (13-4-3) and **John Snavely** (41-8-2) coached undefeated Massillon high school teams, Fugate in 1909 and Snavely in 1916, that aren't recognized as state champions by Massillon historians.

# Cradle of Coaches

*John Snavely*

**Leo Strang** (54-8-1) won three straight state titles (1959-61) and a pair of national titles (1959, 1961). **Earle Bruce** (20-0) produced two state championship teams (1964-65). **Bob Commings** (43-6-2) won Massillon's 22nd high school state title in 1970. Other Massillon coaches have posted impressive records without championship success. **Lee Tressel** (16-3) narrowly missed the state championship in 1957. **Mike Currence** (79-16-2) led Massillon to two state title games (1980, 1982) and three undefeated regular season records. **Lee Owens** (35-13) led Massillon to three straight playoff appearances(1989-91)—twice reaching the semi-finals (1989, 1991). **Jack Rose** (48-17) led Massillon to three playoff appearances (1993-94, 1996) and one regional final (1993).

**"A couple of days after Earle Bruce was here I had the chance** to talk to him privately. I said, 'Earle, you've got to throw the ball here. You can't just run it.' He looked at me like I'd just stuck a dagger through his heart. I thought he was gonna cry."

**Carl "Ducky" Schroeder**

**Legendary Massillon Assistant, 1948-70**

**Massillon Player, 1923**

*—on Massillon fans' love of the passing game.*

**"There's nowhere to hide. In a big city you can get lost. In Massillon** there's nowhere you can get lost. There's no alley dark enough. There's no restaurant you can go to. There's no store you can go to. You don't ever escape being the coach for a minute. That's the hard part. I was always answering questions about the program—all year 'round. It was always on people's minds. Everywhere you'd go in town someone would recognize you, someone would question you."

**Lee Owens**

**Massillon Head Coach, 1988-91**

**Head Coach, Akron University**

*—on the public life of the head coach in Massillon.*

**Legendary Ducky Schroeder had a** profound influence. All of us head coaches probably got more renown, but I think the one guy you most closely associate with Massillon would be Ducky. And it may be out of bounds to say—no, I don't think it's disrespectful to **Paul Brown** to say that at all. They both played here, but Ducky stayed so long."

*Ducky Schroeder*

**Bob Commings**
**Massillon Championship Coach, 1969-1973**
**State Champs, 1970**
**Head Coach, University of Iowa**

*—on the enormous influence of Carl "Ducky" Schroeder.*

*Scribes said it...*

**MASSILLON OUTDRAWS 90% OF NATION'S COLLEGES**
Massillon, which outdraws 90 percent of the nation's colleges at the gate, can afford the best. The coaching and scouting staffs are larger than Cleveland's Big Four colleges combined.

**GORDON COBBLEDICK**
***CLEVELAND PLAIN DEALER*, 1942**

**"We drove through downtown Mansfield in 1949. They had a** banner that said, 'Mansfield State Champs.' Chuck [Mather] was upset. He said, 'We've got to take that sign down.' He said, 'You get on one end and I'll get on the other and we'll start tearing right toward the center.' We got the banner down and threw it in the back seat of the car and drove about a block and a half and stopped at a gas station. The attendant was trying to figure out what was in the back seat. We were laughing. We got gas and got out of there."

**Dave Putts**

**Massillon Assistant, 1948-53**

*—on Mansfield and Massillon's split state titles in the AP and UPI polls.*

**"Mather was the first to use the large squad—90 or 100 players.** And he'd play his subs a lot. Of course he won the state championship every year he was here."

**Luther Emery**

**Legendary Massillon Sportswriter**
**Editor of *The Independent***

*—on Massillon coach Chuck Mather's no-cut policy.*

*Earle Bruce celebrates with captains Don Schenkenberger and John Muhlbach.*

**"It's funny, Earle was 20-0 in Massillon and there are guys who** sit around still, to this day, who criticize Earle for the offense that he ran, because it was too conservative. Yet he was 20-0 and never lost a game. But that's Massillon."

**John Muhlbach**
**All-Ohio Center, 1964**
**Ohio State Center, 1966-68**

*—on the high expectations of Massillon fans.*

**"Earle [Bruce] was a different coach than many we had here.** Earle coached with sort of a fear philosophy—probably the same as **Woody Hayes**. Everybody wondered what would happen if we lost a game. Some of the coaches we had were not like that. They would forget about it after the game. Not only the players, but the assistant coaches were afraid of what would happen if we lost a game. But it brought results—we won all of our games."

**Carl "Ducky" Schroeder**
**Legendary Massillon Assistant, 1948-70**
**Massillon Player, 1923**

*—on Earle Bruce's hold over the players and coaches.*

**"Coach Commings came into the locker room and smacked Kirk Strobel** and punched me. **Willie Spencer** was sitting next to me and started putting his helmet on. I thought, 'I'd better get my butt in gear or else it could be worse when I come back in at the end of the game.' We went back out and won 22-3."

**Tim Ridgley**
**All-Ohio, 1970**

*—on the scene in the Massillon locker room at halftime, trailing Niles 3-0 in 1970.*

**"John Snavely was a good coach. I'd say** the build-up of Massillon football came in his days. They had football before, but the interest started to take over then."

*John Snavely*

## Luther Emery

**Legendary Massillon Sportswriter**
**Editor of *The Independent***

*—on Massillon Head Coach John Snavely (41-8-2) who recorded Massillon's first 10-0 record, in 1916. In 1915, Snavely's Tigers were 9-1, giving up only seven points all season, in a 7-6 season-ending loss to Canton.*

**TIGER TALES**

Massillon won 15 state championships in 20 years, from 1935-54. During that period Massillon won 174 games, losing just 15. The average score: Massillon 32, opponents 5.

**"Bob Seaman made a lot of mistakes. Starting with the All-Star** game, playing his quarterback ahead of (Massillon's) Sheegog. Wearing the Sandusky jacket after taking the Massillon job. A lot of things like that. Boy, you don't do those things. You just don't do those things. He got off on the wrong foot."

**Leo Strang**
**Massillon Championship Head Coach, 1958-63**
**State Champs 1959-61, Nat'l Champs 1959, '61**
**Head Coach, Kent State University**

*—on Head Coach Bob Seaman's start at Massillon. Seamon (20-9-1) coached Massillon from 1966-68.*

**"Mather had the ability to keep people happy and say the right** thing. People would come up to him with a crazy idea and he'd always let 'em talk and he'd listen. He'd say, 'We'll think about that,' then he'd go on about his business. He kept everyone happy. He was a good public relations man and a real good coach."

**Jim Snively**
**Team Dentist**
**School Board President**

*—on head coach Chuck Mather's art of dealing with the Massillon community.*

**"A mother called and said, 'Coach Kammer called my son a horse turd.'** I said, 'I can't believe that.' I talked to Kammer, I said, 'Kammer, I got this call from a mother who said you called her son a horse turd.' He said, 'That's right, he's a horse turd.' I said, 'Why did you have to use *that* expression?' He said, 'Because he's a horse turd.' I said, 'I don't know what you mean.' He said, 'If you would polish a horse turd forever, it would not shine.' "

*Elwood Kammer and John Traylor*

**Chuck Mather**

**Massillon Championship Head Coach, 1948-53**
**Six straight State Titles, Three National Titles**
**Head Coach, University of Kansas**
**Offensive Coordinator, Chicago Bears**

*—on assistant coach Elwood Kammer's unique style.*

**"Vince Lombardi was coaching at Army as an assistant coach. I** remember him sitting in the front row when I spoke at the National Coaches Convention. He actually was intrigued with the [T-formation] sweeping we did at Massillon. You go back to Lombardi—that was his offense at Green Bay."

**Chuck Mather**

**Massillon Championship Head Coach, 1948-53**
**Six Straight State Titles, Three National Titles**
**Head Coach, University of Kansas**
**Offensive Coordinator, Chicago Bears**

*—on the possibility that Vince Lombardi was influenced by Mather's use of the T-formation at Massillon.*

**"Chuck Mather knew how to handle boys. I never heard him yell at a** boy on the field. He always was offering encouragement to the boys and coaches. I think he was the leader in that field. He felt you could win better by encouraging boys than downing them and degrading them."

**Carl "Ducky" Schroeder**

**Legendary Massillon Assistant, 1948-70**
**Massillon Player, 1923**

*—on Chuck Mather's positive attitude.*

**"Ace came up on my porch and said, 'I'm** Ace Grooms and I'd like to go to school in Massillon.' He said he was an all-state end in Pennsylvania, but he was too old to play there. I said, 'Ace, we just couldn't do that, it would be impossible.' Then I went inside and called the football commissioner and told him the story. He said, 'Well, you know Chuck, there's going to be a lot of people investigating this. But if this is all the truth, I don't think you have anything to worry about."

*Ace Grooms*

## Chuck Mather

**Massillon Championship Head Coach, 1948-53**
**Six Straight State Titles, Three National Titles**
**Head Coach, University of Kansas**
**Offensive Coordinator, Chicago Bears**

*—on All-Ohio running back Henry "Ace" Grooms, who gained 1,062 yards—215 against Canton McKinley—and scored the winning touchdown against Steubenville in 1951. Grooms played for Mather at Kansas. No problems ever arose over his transfer to Massillon.*

**"Some coaches left because things didn't work out well, but no coach** could ever leave here and say he didn't have a chance to win. Now that's not true at a lot of places. That's not true at the major college level. In Massillon, as a coach, you are afforded every opportunity to win. You couldn't leave here saying you didn't have a chance to win."

**Bob Commings**
**Massillon Championship Coach, 1969-1973**
**State Champs, 1970**
**Head Coach, University of Iowa**

*—on the opportunity to win at Massillon.*

**"Ducky could talk to you in a manner that you couldn't get mad** at him. Now [Head Coach] Leo [Strang], he could talk to you, but he would kind of scold you. But Ducky, he had a drawn-out voice, he'd tell you just what he had to tell you, then he could take you out there and you would *do* what he wanted you to do."

**Hase McKey**
**2-time 1st Team All-Ohio, 1958-59**
**Arizona State Star**

*—on Massillon assistant coach Carl "Ducky" Schroeder.*

**"Chuck Mather was extremely organized.** Playing quarterback you got to spend a little more time with him. I just idolized those coaches. In fact, that's when I decided to coach."

*Chuck Mather*

**Don James**

**Massillon Championship Quarterback, 1949**
**Record-breaking Quarterback, Univ. of Miami**
**Nat'l Championship Coach, Univ. of Washington, 1991**

*—on his Massillon coaches' influence on his career.*

**"Chuck Mather was a hero, an absolute hero. Obviously when we** started football in seventh grade we had one goal in life—to play for the Massillon Tigers and to play under Chuck Mather. He was a god, he was an idol of everyone's."

**David Canary**

**All-Ohio, 1956**
**All-American, University of Cincinnati, 1959**
**4-Time Emmy Winner, "All My Children"**
**Played "Candy" on "Bonanza"**

*—on his feelings about head coach Chuck Mather (57-3), who won six straight state titles at Massillon.*

**"Mike Currence was 0-2, and there aren't many coaches who** go 0-2 and remain real popular at Massillon. But then he went on to win his last eight and beat McKinley and turned out to be one of our great coaches."

**John Muhlbach**

**All-Ohio Center, 1964**
**Academic All Big 10, Ohio State University, 1968**
**Booster Club President, 1976**

*—on the rocky start of coach Mike Currence (79-16-2).*

**"Massillon was the first team in the United States to wear white shoes—** that made them look sharp. We were the first to put decals on the helmet—the leaping tiger. We started the helmet award system, too—putting stars on the helmet."

**Leo Strang**

**Massillon Championship Head Coach, 1958-63**
**State Champs, 1959-61, Nat'l Champs 1959, '61**
**Head Coach, Kent State University**

*—on three football innovations he started at Massillon.*

**"I occasionally have a dream that I've gone back there to coach. And** I'm feeling desperate as to whether we're going to win or not. It's like starting new. Every once in a while I dream I'm back in Massillon to coach, and I don't know if we're good enough or anything like that. Sure don't want to lose."

**Chuck Mather**

**Massillon Championship Head Coach, 1948-53**
**Six Straight State Titles, Three National Titles**
**Head Coach, University of Kansas**
**Offensive Coordinator, Chicago Bears**

*—on dreams he has about returning to Massillon to coach.*

**"The phone rang--it was April first. I know April first is April** fools day. It was late at night. And the party on the other end says, 'This is L.J. Smith. We've heard some fine things about you and we wonder if you'd be interested in coming up to Massillon for an interview.' I said, 'Yeah, yeah, April Fools.' I thought it was my neighbor. L.J. laughed, 'It *is* April Fools, but this *is* L.J. Smith.' I had no choice but to go along with him.'"

**Tom Harp**

**Massillon Championship Head Coach, 1954-55**
**State Champs, 1954**
**Head Coach Duke, Cornell, Indiana State**
**Assistant to Colonel Blake at Army**

*—on being contacted about the coaching job at Massillon.*

**"Bob Commings made a statement when he left here, he said, 'People, don't lose it. Let 'em criticize you.** Let 'em tell you that all you have is football. But you know what? Some towns ain't got nothin'. He was the truest Tiger you ever wanted to see."

**Phil Glick**

**Team Historian**

*—on the Massillon coach's parting words.*

*Two-time All-Ohioan Hase McKey with coach Leo Strang. Strang was the first to put plastic decals on helmets.*

**"We loved Leo's style. The way he liked the guys to dress. Everybody** loved that. Not only did you play good, you looked good doing it. Everybody wanted to go out and play. Because on Friday night, those guys looked good."

**David Whitfield**

**All-Ohio 1965**

**Captain, Ohio State, 1970**

*—on Head Coach Leo Strang's flashy style.*

**"I was horrified. I didn't know what the town's reaction was going to** be. Were they going to fire me? I didn't know what they were going to do. I said, 'I'm here, that's it. We'll do what we have to do. I'm young. My life's not going to come to an end.' I remember getting up in front of the squad on Monday night. I said, 'O.K., we lost a game. We didn't play well. We didn't deserve to win. Give them credit. Our goal now is to win the state championship.' "

**Tom Harp**

**Massillon Championship Head Coach, 1954-55**
**State Champs, 1954**
**Head Coach Duke, Cornell, Indiana State**
**Assistant to Colonel Blake at Army**

*—on losing for the first time at Massillon. His '54 team rebounded to win the State Championship.*

**"Chuck Mather could get a little emotional at times during the** game. **Elwood Kammer** would sometimes step in and smooth things over and run the show."

**Dick Cordes**

**Massillon Player, 1950**

*—on the assistant coach's calming influence. Kammer was a championship head coach for Massillon in 1943.*

*Tom Harp considers advice against McKinley, 1954.*

**"One of my goals was to maintain,** and if possible build upon that great tradition at Massillon. **Paul Brown** had it. **Chuck Mather** had it. I wanted to have the same thing."

## Tom Harp

**Massillon Championship Head Coach, 1954-55**
**State Champs, 1954**
**Head Coach Duke, Cornell, Indiana State**
**Assistant to Colonel Blake at Army**

*—on following Chuck Mather's 57-3 run at Massillon.*

**"Every coach who ever comes in here is coming into a different level.** They were all the same, they weren't ready. This is another step up from wherever they've been. They weren't scouted as well, they didn't have as many teams 'point' toward them and they didn't have the level of community involvement that they have here. In Massillon you're not just head coach, you have to take care of the community's interests. I don't think there's any place like this."

**Dale Walterhouse**

**Longtime Massillon Assistant**

*—on the Massillon experience for new head coaches.*

**"Chuck Mather was the first coach to grade movies with a** computer. He was the first to have a television on the sidelines— he had the television right beside him. He was the first to show movies of the first quarter at halftime in the locker room."

**Carl "Ducky" Schroeder**

**Legendary Massillon Assistant, 1948-70**

**Massillon Player, 1923**

*—on innovations by Chuck Mather. The sideline television and halftime films were later banned.*

# The Rivalry

## ONE OF THE GREAT RIVALRIES IN SPORTS HISTORY

The Massillon versus Canton McKinley high school football rivalry started in 1894. A combined 28 State Championships and 11 National Championships later, these high school powers continue to square off before capacity crowds of 20,000 every November.

The intense rivalry actually began in the early days of professional football. Massillon won pro championships from 1903-07; Canton in 1922-23.

When both teams left the professional ranks, their high school rivalry became as intense as their professional rivalry was, when the "Fix of '06" gave professional football its first scandal.

On many occasions the outcome of the Massillon-Canton game has decided state, national or professional championships. Today's games are just as hard fought as the ones 30, 40, 50—even 90 years ago. And it doesn't look like things are going to to change soon.

**"You know, the week of the game there's not a helluva lot on anybody's** mind but the [Massillon-McKinley] game. The topic of conversation—that's about it. So much is brought up about the tradition and history and former games and former players—and there's a little hatred mixed in there—competitive hatred. You don't want to lose to these guys if you lose to anybody."

**Don James**

**Massillon Championship Quarterback, 1949**
**Record-breaking Quarterback, Univ. of Miami**
**Nat'l Championship Coach, Univ. of Washington, 1991**

*—on Massillon-McKinley week.*

**"While I was here coaching we played McKinley 23 times. We won 18 and lost five.** I think most of the credit has to go to the Massillon community and the kids we had on the football teams. They really die by inches, as Paul Brown says."

**Carl "Ducky" Schroeder**

**Legendary Massillon Assistant, 1948-70**
**Massillon Player, 1923**

*—on his success against Canton McKinley.*

**"I would compare McKinley Week to, as a coach out at Washington,** getting ready to play USC or the Rose Bowl or the Orange Bowl—not just any Bowl—one of the big ones, where there's so much on the line and so much visibility involved."

**Don James**

**Massillon Championship Quarterback, 1949**
**Record-Breaking Quarterback, Univ. of Miami**
**Nat'l Championship Coach, Univ. of Washington, 1991**

*—on McKinley week.*

**"Mather grabbed Al Brown by the shoulder pads and said, 'You better** tell those guys we've gotta take the ball all the way and score a touchdown.' Al came back to the huddle and said, 'If you guys don't do it I'm going to kick every one of your asses.' We drove 80 yards and scored a touchdown."

**Jack Hill**

**Massillon Quarterback, 1946-48**
**Booster Club President, 1967**

*—on Massillon's final drive, and their fiery captain Al Brown, in their 21-12 win over McKinley in 1948.*

**"We came down to the McKinley game and they're ranked #1 and** we're ranked #2. They were favored. It wasn't even close. We just kicked the tar out of them. I mean, we beat 'em 26-6 and it could have been 40-6. We dominated 'em."

**Tom Harp**

**Massillon Championship Head Coach, 1954-55**
**State Champs, 1954**
**Head Coach Duke, Cornell, Indiana State**
**Assistant to Colonel Blake at Army**

*—on winning the 1954 State Championship.*

**"I was the secret weapon against McKinley. Leo sat me** out and didn't say anything to me for three weeks. I wondered why I was sitting on the bench for those three games. The week of the McKinley game they told me why. They were setting it up so McKinley would key on **Bill Blunt** out of the tailback position. It turned out McKinley *did* key on Blunt and that left me open. I ran for over 100 yards and scored twice."

**Terry Getz**

**Massillon Running Back, 1961-63**

*—on Massillon's 22-6 win, one of two over McKinley in 1963.*

*Larry Harper*

**"John Bride-weiser said that he can't get over the impulse he felt** when he knew that **Larry Harper** wasn't going to be caught. As he was running by him he swore that Harper looked at him and smiled. He had coached Larry the year before at Massillon. His impulse was to tackle the little rascal and get him on the ground. Fortunately for Johnny he didn't try it. The opening kickoff—it really was a cruise for Larry, because we kind of tricked 'em on it."

## Bob Commings

**Massillon Championship Coach, 1969-1973**
**State Champs, 1970**
**Head Coach, University of Iowa**

*—on Larry Harper's opening kickoff return for a touchdown that started Massillon's 28-0 win over McKinley.*

**"In high school football there's no way that any game compares** to Massillon-McKinley, I don't care what anybody tells me."

**Chris Spielman**

**Massillon: 2-time All-Ohioan, All-American,**
**USA Today Defensive Player of the Year, 1983**
**Ohio State: 2-time All-American,**
**Lombardi Award Winner**
**NFL: Detroit Lions, Buffalo Bills, Since1988**
**4-time Pro Bowl**

*—on the Massillon-McKinley game.*

**"They tell you, 'You'll never forget it. You'll go to your grave** remembering this [Massillon-McKinley] game.' People just beat you up with that stuff. And you start to believe it—and then you find it's true."

**Don James**

**Massillon Championship Quarterback, 1949**
**Record-breaking Quarterback, Univ. of Miami**
**National Championship Coach, 1991**
**University of Washington**

*—on the Massillon-McKinley game.*

*Earl Martin flies through the air, vainly trying to block a punt against Canton McKinley in 1938.*

**"I missed the damned thing. I can't believe that I missed it. He shanked** it. You'd swear that I had that kick. My shoulder was injured and I could only get my arm so high."

**Earl "Ick" Martin**

**Captain, All-Ohio Center**
**1939 State Championship Team**

*—on a kick he nearly blocked against McKinley.*

***Scribes said it...***

Football, they seem to believe, is a religion, a cult, an infectious disease of epidemic proportions, and in fact, a complete way of life.

**JEROME BRONDFIELD**
***SPORT MAGAZINE,* 1950**

**"When I was 8 years old my father said, 'It's about time you see a football** game.' Massillon High was playing Canton. They played in the back of North Street School, where Longfellow School now stands. The football field wasn't long enough to have two goal posts, they just had a goal post at one end of the field. The score was 13-13. The year was 1913."

**Luther Emery**

**Legendary Massillon Sportswriter**
**Editor of *The Independent***

*—on his first memory of Massillon football.*

**"People say I knocked Mariano out. Actually, I couldn't get away from** him. If I could have moved or ducked I probably would have. But I didn't have a chance. When I looked up this guy's on top of me. He was on his way in."

**Irvin "Ace" Crable**

**Legendary Massillon Running Back**
**All-Ohio, Stark County Player of the Year, 1949**

*—on Crable's game-saving tackle that caused Lou Mariano to fumble. Massillon recovered. Crable also scored the game's only points on a 35-yard touchdown run.*

**"I got tackled out of bounds against McKinley and I was stunned for a** couple of seconds. Coach Commings told the Booster Club that he came over to see if I was all right. He said that I asked him how the crowd was taking it before I got up. He was a funny guy. I never said that."

**Willie Spencer**

**All-Ohio Running Back, 1971**
**World Football League Star, 1974-75, Memphis**
**NFL Running Back: Minnesota Vikings, Washington Redskins, New York Giants**

*—on head coach Bob Commings's sense of humor.*

**"The only thing better than beating McKinley is beating them twice."**

**John Muhlbach**

**All-Ohio Center, 1964**
**Academic All Big 10, 1968**
**Booster Club President, 1976**

*—on the 1963 Tigers (9-1), the first Massillon team to beat Canton McKinley twice in one season.*

**"When you lose here it's almost like a death. Especially if you lose to McKinley."**

**Jack Rose**

**Massillon Head Coach, 1992-97**

*—on losing to McKinley. Rose was 1-6 against the Bulldogs.*

**"The play was 33 cross. Don James handed the ball to me, and all I could** see was daylight—and I fumbled it. Later, in the fourth quarter, the coach sent in the play. I said, 'Don, no. Let's run 33 cross.' And he changed the play. The way the hole opened the first time—it happened the same way the second time. And that was that. The line blocking was beautiful—nobody had a chance. Nobody laid a hand on me. My instincts told me it was going to be there again. I waited and waited. Then I thought, now's the time. It was right there again. I ran right into the end zone."

**Irvin "Ace" Crable**

**Legendary Massillon Running Back**
**All-Ohio, Stark County Player of the Year, 1949**

*—on Crable's 35 yard touchdown run that beat McKinley 6-0 in 1949.*

**"You talk to people, they revert back to that 1964 game. They** say 'I remember that game. You came in and beat Canton McKinley single-handed.' I didn't beat 'em single-handed. The plays worked. The blocks. And we ended up winning. It became the greatest comeback in the history of the Massillon-McKinley rivalry. Both teams were 9-0, playing for the championship. A lot of people will always remember that. It was a super outstanding game, to come back and win it when the first three quarters everything was McKinley."

**David Sheegog**

**Star Massillon Quarterback, 1964-65**

*—on Sheegog coming off the bench to lead Massillon to three fourth-quarter touchdowns and a 20-14 win.*

**"I remember the rush onto the field, sliding in the mud. Nick Vrotsos and** I hugging and rolling in the mud. Yelling back at the stands, 'I love Massillon.' "

**Lee Owens**

**Massillon Head Coach, 1988-91**
**Head Coach, Akron University**

*—on Massillon's 10-7 overtime win over Canton McKinley in 1988—the first overtime game in the series.*

**"That 1934 game was *the* game. That was the one that started it.** The game has been nearly a sellout ever since. Never had a sellout before."

**Luther Emery**

**Legendary Massillon Sportswriter**
**Editor of *The Independent***

*—on the 1934 Massillon-McKinley game, played before an estimated crowd of 22,000 people at Massillon Field on Shriver Street. McKinley won, 21-6.*

**"It was a lot easier than I expected it to be because the holes were** there—our line was making the holes. You'd break through the line and you couldn't believe you were that wide open at times. McKinley was number one in the state and they were so much larger than we were. We thought they were going to be one tough game. It was a tough game, I was just surprised the holes were so big."

**Homer Floyd**

**Legendary Massillon running back, 1952-54,**
**All-Ohio, 1954**
**University of Kansas star, 1955-58**

*—on the 1954 Massillon-McKinley game. Massillon won, 26-6. Floyd gained 263 yards.*

**"I just remember the buildup, from the student body to the pep rallies** and the press. It was almost bigger than life. And honestly, I don't think in college—our big game was Florida—I was ever as excited as the Canton McKinley game."

**Don James**

**Massillon Championship Quarterback, 1949**
**Record-Breaking Quarterback, Univ. of Miami**
**Nat'l Championship Coach, Univ. of Washington, 1991**

*—on Massillon-McKinley week.*

**"The McKinley week in Massillon is a week that is hard to describe.** A lot of schools try to duplicate that with other great rivalries, but I'm not sure any of them really reach the magnitude you find in Massillon/McKinley."

**Jim Reichenbach**

**All-Ohio, 1950**
**All-American, Ohio State, 1954**

*—on Massillon-McKinley week.*

**"The Dive. People make a big deal out of that. I did that on instinct.** The hole was so wide open I could have walked over. I saw the opening and the quickest way to get there was to dive. But I used that a lot. I used it in the World Football League and I used it in the NFL."

**Willie Spencer**

**All-Ohio Running Back, 1971**
**World Football League Star, 1974-75, Memphis**
**NFL Running Back: Minnesota Vikings, Washington Redskins, New York Giants**

*—on Spencer's diving touchdown in Massillon's 29-6 win over Canton McKinley in 1971.*

**"Tim Gutshall told a reporter after Massillon upset McKinley in 1974,** 'Massillon is not a town of athletes. It's a town of football players.' What a profound statement out of a 17-year-old. And that's what we are. We have talent—but most of our long years of success are because we are a town of football players."

**Phil Glick**

**Team Historian**

*—on Tiger Captain Tim Gutshall's answer to a post-game question about whether Canton McKinley had better athletes than Massillon in 1974.*

## “We demoralized McKinley when we came out for the second half

*Mike Mauger*

with brand new uniforms on. It was so muddy, which was an advantage to us because I ran so well in the mud. I always liked running in it. When we got in the locker room the coaches were yelling, ‘Everybody get your uniforms off, put new ones on.’ I actually changed everything. We came out at halftime clean and fresh. Which demoralized McKinley. It was cold—halfway between rain and snow.”

**Mike Mauger**

**All-Ohio Running Back, 1970**

*—on the 1970 McKinley game, a 28-0 Massillon win.*

### *Scribes said it...*

Massillon is Football Town—in capital letters. It’s the only city in the nation where the Ladies’ Aid can give you offhand the weights of this year’s backfield and the score of the big Thanksgiving Day game 20 years ago.

**WATSON FENIMORE, *PATHFINDER* MAGAZINE, 1947**

**"Bob Commings told the players, 'Some of you are going to play in** college, and you'll have big games. Some of you might even play in the pros, and you'll have big games. But you'll never have a game like you're going to have Saturday. It will be the most important you'll ever play in. First of all, you're going to play for yourself. You've *gotta* play for yourself. When you go to college you're going to play for your school. You go to the pros, you're playing for money. Saturday, you're going to play for your town. Forty years from now, when you go in to have a beer with your buddies, they're not going to care what you did in college, how much money you made in the pros. They're gonna know what you did in the McKinley game your senior year.'"

**Junie Studer**

**Massillon Tiger Sign Painter**
**Booster Club President, 1972**

*—on Massillon Head Coach Bob Commings' inspirational speech before a Wednesday practice in 1972.*

*Scribes said it...*

If your spine doesn't tingle, if you fail to see footballs in your sleep, if you don't feel just a little different during McKinley week, you're not a dyed-in-the-wool Massillon football fan.

**LUTHER EMERY, *THE EVENING INDEPENDENT*, 1948**

**"You always think about having that big game against McKinley**

growing up, playing in the yard. You know, as a kid you pretend the game's on the line, you're on the two yard line, you're Chris Spielman, something like that. But to rush for 300 yards in front of that many people, and score five touchdowns. To gain 300 yards in the biggest game of your life, it's kind of overwhelming."

*Travis McGuire*

## Travis McGuire

**All-Ohio Running Back, 1991**
**Stark County Player of the Year, 1991**
**Ohio Offensive Player of the Year, 1991**

*—on a dream coming true against Canton McKinley. McGuire rushed for 302 yards in the 42-13 win in 1991.*

**"The McKinley pep rally was always special. Townspeople would come** over for it. The bonfire on Friday night for the town was great. The parade, you got to ride on the truck through town. That's how Massillon kids are raised. They prepare their whole life for that game. They look forward to that. It's their time to shine."

**Chris Spielman**

**Massillon: 2-time All-Ohioan, All-American,**
**USA Today Defensive Player of the Year, 1983**
**Ohio State: 2-time All-American,**
**Lombardi Award Winner**
**NFL: Detroit Lions, Buffalo Bills, Since 1988**
**Four Pro Bowls**

*—on Massillon-McKinley week.*

**"I can tell you how Brown scouted McKinley back then. They sent 11** scouts to every game McKinley played. If you had the right tackle, you wrote down every movement he made. Now that's detail. One man on each guy—and you better have on your report what he did on each play."

**Earl "Ick" Martin**

**Captain, All-Ohio Center**
**1939 State Championship Team**

*—on the thoroughness of Paul Brown's preparation.*

**"We played McKinley at Lehman Stadium in 1937 and it was a sea** of mud. The temperature was 15 or 20 degrees. The field was just mud, no grass on it. We'd play on one end of the field and it would be muddy. The next time you came down there the mud would be frozen, it was so cold. We had one muddy ball. At halftime my two fingers were frozen—frostbitten. We washed 'em off in cold water and finished the game. We beat 'em [19-6]. That's where I almost lost some of my desire to play football."

**Earl "Ick" Martin**

**Captain, All-Ohio Center**
**1939 State Championship Team**

*—on playing center against McKinley as a sophomore.*

**"It was butchering day. We were listening to the Massillon-McKinley** game while we were butchering hogs. I remember I was impressed by the sound of the crowd. That was my first exposure to Massillon football."

**Lee Nussbaum**

**All-Ohio running back, 1952**

*—on his first childhood memory of Massillon football.*

**"They were ahead of us 14-0 going into halftime [in 1965]. When I** walked in the locker room, I was really down. I mean I was *down.* To think that we're down 14 to *nuthin'*. I look at **Ducky Schroeder** and I say, 'Holy man are we playing bad. Ducky said, 'Coach, we've got another half.' I said, 'Ducky, you don't come back two years in a row against a team like Canton McKinley.' Ducky said, 'Massillon can do it, coach.' I said, 'My God Ducky, the odds are tremendous this won't happen.' We went back out and won 18-14."

**Earle Bruce**

**Championship Coach, 1964-65**
**State Champs, #2 in Nation, 1964-65**
**Head Coach, Ohio State University**

*—on his halftime discussion with legendary assistant Carl "Ducky" Schroeder during the 1965 McKinley game.*

*Scribes said it...*

**Jim Thorpe** showed a keen interest in the rivalry between Canton and Massillon and was amazed at the Tigers' record. "You people in Canton should do everything possible to help beat that Massillon bunch," he laughed. "When I played here, there was no limit to what we would do to whip Massillon."

**HARRY YOCKEY, *THE CANTON REPOSITORY,* 1940**

**"Marion Motley, they shut him down real good [in 1938] down** on what I call the "old field." In fact he went out of the game injured. Didn't return. I think **Bud Lucius** hit him real hard. He didn't get knocked out of a game in Cleveland in all those years."

**Tommy James**

**All-Ohio halfback, 1940**
**Ohio State Captain-Elect, 1946**
**Member of Cleveland Browns All-Time Team**

*—on the 1938 Massillon-McKinley game.*

**"The pressure you feel that morning of the day you play Canton** McKinley. How everybody wants to win that game so much. You feel a responsibility, an accountability, being the coach. You try to find a way to make it happen. And how terrible you feel when it doesn't happen—not just for yourself but for the community. They kind of build their sense of worth around that game."

**Lee Owens**

**Massillon Head Coach, 1988-91**
**Head Coach, Akron University**

*—on the pressure of the Massillon-McKinley game. Owens was 3-1 against McKinley.*

**"It was just like Super Bowl week on a smaller scale. It was so crazy.** That's one crazy week. It wasn't like you could prepare for the game. There were so many distractions. I was just like, 'Let's just play football.' But I really enjoyed it.' "

**Tom Hannon**

**All-Ohio, 1972**
**Two-time All-Big 10, Michigan State, 1975-76**
**Minnesota Vikings Star, 1977-83**

*—on Massillon/McKinley week.*

**As soon as Nick Pribich made the kick, Coach Steve Studer and I sprinted across** the field, we both grabbed the bell and brought it back over to the Massillon side. It felt great. Up to that point, I didn't think that much of it. But now, every time I watch a replay of the game it shows me and Coach Studer walking with the bell. It brings tears to my eyes. The end of that game makes me feel so good inside."

**Willie Spencer, Jr.**

**All-Ohio Quarterback, 1994**

*—on the victory bell which goes to the winner of the Massillon-McKinley game. Spencer led Massillon to a 42-41 overtime victory in 1994.*

# Paul E. Brown

## MANY SAY PAUL E. BROWN *IS* MASSILLON FOOTBALL. FOR CERTAIN, HIS IMPRESSION IS UNDENIABLE—AND INDELIBLE

Paul Brown became a legend in football at Massillon, winning championships and creating a fervor for football. His legend grew as he won Ohio State's first national championship in 1942—and Ohio State became like Massillon. The Cleveland Browns, named after Paul Brown, enjoyed unparalleled success, —and they became like Massillon. When Paul Brown formed the Cincinnati Bengals and led them to a Super Bowl faster than any other expansion team—they, too became like Massillon.

Paul Brown wove the Massillon "thread" through his entire career. And everywhere he went he tried to create "another Massillon." Arguably the finest coach in football history, a national champion at every level of football, Paul Brown loved Massillon as much as Massillon loved him. And he left Massillon in a state of football delirium that will last forever.

**"We are all useful, but none of us are necessary."**

**"Doc" Bell**

**President of the School Board**
**Massillon Doctor**

*—on advice he gave to Paul Brown.*

**"Paul never complimented you. *Never.* A lot of people resented that. I didn't."**

**Shirley Bird**

**Band Director George "Red" Bird's Daughter**
**Cincinnati Bengals Entertainment Director**

*—on Paul Brown's leadership style.*

**"When he was really famous and very successful, he never forgot his** friends in Massillon. You just can't imagine how tickled he was to see you and how anxious he was to do something for you."

**Tom McConnaughy**

**Massillon Industrial Arts Teacher**
**Childhood Friend of Paul Brown**

*—on his dealings with Paul Brown as an adult.*

**"Mansfield tied us 6-6 in '37. That didn't ride well with Brown.** In 1938 we went up there and beat 'em 33-7, but that wasn't revenge enough. So when they came down here in '39, the first team stayed in the whole damn game because he was pissed off at that coach for tying us. We beat 'em 73-0."

**Earl "Ick" Martin**

**Captain, All-Ohio Center**
**1939 State Championship Team**

*—on one of the toughest games he played at Massillon.*

**"Don't miss practice. There was no excuse. And don't stay out of** school—or you'd hear it from **Paul Brown.** You'd hear it from all the coaches—the players, too. Brown would make *them* work harder. If you miss a day, you're going to make up for it— because he was mad that you missed it. You didn't miss practice with Paul Brown, because you'd catch hell from him *and* the players."

**Odell Gillom**

**Massillon End, 1935-36**
**One of Massillon's famous Gillom Brothers**

*—on Paul Brown's strictness about practice and school.*

**"Quite often Paul would stop by and watch our practices at Longfellow.** **Horace Gillom** was in eighth grade. I told him, 'I tried to teach him a step and a half to punt, but he can't kick it worth a damn.' He said, 'Well, keep doing it.' So I kept working with him, and finally I said, 'If you want to use him as a punter you have to let him take three steps. Just put him back further.' So we put him back 15 yards. That extra five yards didn't make any difference to him. One time, in our junior high game, he kicked the ball 85 yards in the air—in a junior high game."

**Bud Houghton**

**Championship Head Coach, 1941, 1946-47**
**State Champs, 1941**
**Massillon Player, 1925-26**

*—on Horace Gillom, Massillon's All-Ohio End who became one of the best punters in professional football history.*

**"He'd say, 'That's piss poor. I know it can be done. I can do it better myself.' "**

**Ray Getz**

**All-Ohio 1939, Co-Captain 1940**

*—on Paul Brown's reaction to sloppy play.*

**"Brown's methods were the same from high school to college to the** pros, so it was easy for me to follow him. I knew more what to expect, how he held his practices, better than some rookie coming in from college into pro ball. I went to college at Ohio State and he ran his practices just like he did here in Massillon."

*Paul E. Brown*

## Tommy James

**All-Ohio Halfback, 1940**
**Ohio State Captain-Elect, 1946**
**Member of Cleveland Browns All-Time Team**

*—on playing football for Paul Brown.*

**"Paul loved Massillon. Massillon was everything to him. He'd say,** 'When I die I want to go back to Massillon,' and that's where he came back to."

## Marian Evans

**Coach Paul Brown's Sister**

*—on her brother's wish.*

**"Well, I was like any other young kid, I was like, in awe. You had heard so** much about him. I would say just the word *awe,* that you got to know the man and play for him. As a freshman we heard all about it. We knew what the varsity was doing as freshmen in school. We got invited down to our first practice. We knew right then that he was going to keep the players he thought were best. You had to continually strive to do better to make the squad."

**Tommy James**

**All-Ohio Halfback, 1940**
**Ohio State Captain-Elect, 1947**
**Member of Cleveland Browns All-Time Team**

*—on his first contact with Paul Brown.*

**"His way was a fantastic way to do it. He came right to the point. He** didn't flower any speeches. He just came to exact words. He knew certain words, whether it was cutting, complimentary, to make you work harder or that he means business."

**Mike Byelene**

**All-Ohio, Captain, 1936**
**Record-setting Quarterback, Purdue**

*—on Paul Brown as a communicator.*

**"When we won the state title, that's the only time I ever saw him laugh and have a good time."**

*Jimmy Aiken (l) and Paul Brown.*

**Augie Morningstar**

**All-Ohio, Captain, 1935**
**Head Coach, Massillon, 1945**
**Championship Head Coach, Mansfield, 1949**

*—on Coach Brown, following his first win over Canton McKinley and coach Jimmy Aiken in 1935.*

**"Paul Brown said, 'You, *you* thought that we were going to run** all over New Castle.' I said, 'Yeah, but I didn't know the right side of your line was going to be out.' That's the only words I ever had with Paul. He was madder than a hornet. He was undefeated in 1935, undefeated in 1936 and undefeated in 1937, until that ball game."

**Luther Emery**

**Legendary Massillon Sportswriter**
**Editor of *The Independent***

*—on Paul Brown following a 7-0 loss to New Castle, PA.*

**"The intensity, that was always there. The ability to organize. The ability to express himself forcefully, succinctly—that impressed players over a 50 year span."**

**Mike Brown**

**Coach Paul Brown's Son**
**General Manager, Cincinnati Bengals**

*—on themes that carried throughout his father's life.*

**"I was so obsessed with it, I don't think I really knew my own limitations."**

**Paul E. Brown**

**Massillon Quarterback, 1923-25**
**Championship Coach: Massillon Tigers, Ohio State Buckeyes and Cleveland Browns**
**Coach of 14 Championship teams**
**Founder, Head Coach, GM, Cincinnati Bengals**

*—on himself as a junior quarterback at Massillon.*

**"They wouldn't give me a uniform for football. Which is quite a blow** to this "great" player. They just took one look at me. I weighed about 150 pounds."

**Paul E. Brown**

**Massillon Quarterback, 1923-25**
**Championship Coach: Massillon Tigers, Ohio State Buckeyes and Cleveland Browns**
**Coached 14 Championship Teams**
**Founder of the Cincinnati Bengals**

*—on his try-out at Ohio State University.*

**"He didn't want you to have a girlfriend. Even Charlie Anderson,** he was one of the roughest ones on the team—he would break more rules than anybody else. I don't even remember *him* having a girlfriend."

**Edgar "Echo" Herring**

**Massillon's #6 All-Time Scorer (215 points) 1934-36**

*—on Paul Brown's rule against players dating.*

**"I wouldn't say I loved him. I respected him. Just like anybody** who's got you under his thumb. You bitch. Cuss him out under your breath. I respected him, though. He was always fair. I would say I don't think any of the players loved him. They respected him. I could be wrong. Thought a lot of him, the players. I would never use the word love. Respect, yes. Like, yes."

**Tommy James**

**All-Ohio Halfback, 1940**
**Ohio State Captain-Elect, 1946**
**Member of Cleveland Browns All-Time Team**

*—on whether he loved coach Paul Brown, his coach in high school, college and professional football.*

**"Brown told me he was going to copy New York University coach Chic Meehan's** offense—which was a military shift. They would line-up, 'hup two, hup three,' kind of military-like. They gave that up after one year."

**Luther Emery**

**Legendary Massillon Sportswriter**
**Editor of *The Independent***

*—on a conversation with Paul Brown after he was named head coach at Massillon, 1932.*

**"Paul Brown was a bad man—I mean it was built that way. Hugh** McGranahan and Carol Widdoes were the pals of the players. Paul would go in and chew somebody out—or chew the team out, turn around and walk away. Then the pacifiers would come in. McGranahan, Widdoes. 'Now boys, now boys, now the old man's mad. But this is what we've gotta do. Come on now, we gotta do this, let's make the old man happy.' It was beautiful to watch it work."

**Bob Immel**

**Student Manager, 1934-37**
**Booster Club President, 1956**
**School Board President**
**Team Dentist**

*—on Paul Brown and assistants Widdoes and McGranahan.*

**"Paul was funny. He was strict. And he would kick guys off the team** at times. But he never kicked a regular off the team."

**Bob Immel**

**Student Manager, 1934-37**
**Booster Club President, 1956**
**School Board President**
**Team Dentist**

*—on Paul Brown as a disciplinarian.*

**"Coach Clay, he was a farmer. He came to practice a half-hour late.** **Paul Brown** said, 'Where you been, what's the trouble? You were supposed to be here at 3 o'clock. We don't need you now. You get the hell out of here. We don't want you anymore. Your interest is elsewhere. Go take care of your farm.' Fired him right now. I was in junior high then. That straightened me out. I thought, man this guy means business. What he says goes."

**Mike Byelene**

**All-Ohio, Captain, 1936**
**Record-Setting Quarterback, Purdue**

*—on a practice he observed at Jones School in 1933.*

**"He could be very sharp, even cutting, and he could do it in a word and a half, it seemed like."**

**Mike Brown**

**Coach Paul Brown's Son**
**General Manager, Cincinnati Bengals**

*—on his father's style.*

**"I feel honored. I like to drive out there and just look at it."**

**Paul E. Brown**

**Massillon Quarterback, 1923-25**
**Championship Coach: Massillon Tigers, Ohio State Buckeyes and Cleveland Browns**
**Coached 14 Championship Teams**
**Founder, Head Coach, GM, Cincinnati Bengals**

*—on his feelings about Tiger Stadium bearing his name.*

**"I asked Paul Brown what he was going to do different. He said, 'We** won't be using the water bucket.' It used to be every time out someone would run with the water bucket and a dipper. 'And the team will stand during all intermissions. They will not sit down and rest.' He got that from **Chic Meehan** (NYU coach). 'Chick also had them jump over a rope when they came off of the field. But I'm not going to do that.' "

**Luther Emery**

**Legendary Massillon Sportswriter**
**Editor of *The Independent***

*—on a conversation with Paul Brown after he was named head coach at Massillon, 1932.*

**"He had this standard, and if you didn't live up to it, it didn't matter** who you were, you had to go. And there was never any remorse about it with him. If a person had failed to live up to his duty, he was gone. For the good of the team, he was gone."

**Mike Brown**

**Coach Paul Brown's Son**
**General Manager, Cincinnati Bengals**

*—on his father's unwavering standard.*

**"Paul Brown, he'd go around, bite his lip.** He wouldn't say what was on his mind—probably would have exploded."

**Mike Byelene**

**All-Ohio, Captain, 1936**
**Record-Setting quarterback, Purdue**

*—on the angriest he's seen Paul Brown.*

**"He always wore white pants at Massillon. And he didn't wash them—didn't want to wash the winning out of them."**

Paul E. Brown

## Augie Morningstar

**All-Ohio, Captain, 1935**
**Head Coach, Massillon, 1945**
**Championship Head Coach**
**Mansfield, 1949**

*—on a superstition of Paul Brown's while he coached at Massillon.*

**TIGER TALES**

August 9, 1939

Dear Red—

Just a word to remind you that it won't be long now—you plan on hard work—the one we really want to lick is Canton!

P.E.B.

**A POSTCARD: PAUL BROWN TO TOMMY JAMES**

**"Brown called us all in, the players and the parents. He said, 'We're** going to pick the best players, regardless of who they are.' He meant race or whether your parents had money. Paul Brown was strong in his ideas. He was fair. He just told 'em that's how it was going to be. He told the parents that the best players were going to play football, regardless of who they are or where they come from. He just got it straight that he was going to run the show without any outside interference. And that's the way he stuck to it."

**Tommy James**

**All-Ohio Halfback, 1940**
**Ohio State Captain-Elect, 1946**
**Member of Cleveland Browns All-Time Team**

*—on his first team meeting with Paul Brown in 1938.*

*Scribes said it...*

Paul Brown took me for a drive around Massillon. We passed a grade school at recess time. Out in the school yard were 30 or 40 boys. It was snowing, and those kids were running around in heavy coats and galoshes. And what was the toy they were playing with? You guessed it—a football!

**MICHAEL DESMOND**
***THE COLUMBUS CITIZEN*, 1940**

**"Someone had turned "Buut" Anderson in for being out late. Paul** Brown always had a meeting before practice. Everybody was there. Buut's already there, ready to practice. He has his uniform on. Brown says, 'Buut Anderson, you were seen at such and such a place at this time in the morning, and as of this time your football career is over.' He would not allow Anderson to say a word. Nothing. He had to take off his uniform and he was done playing.' "

*Charlie Anderson*

## Earl "Ick" Martin

**Captain, All-Ohio Center**
**1939 State Championship Team**

*—on Brown's dismissal of his former Massillon star, Charley "Buut" Anderson, from the Ohio State squad.*

### *Scribes said it...*

Paul Brown is a showman, too. His boys come on the field in batches of 11 and jog its length, flipping the football. They are flashily uniformed. The equipment bill would wreck a small college in a couple of years.

**BEN WILLIAMSON, *CLEVELAND PLAIN DEALER,* 1939**

**"Dr. Bell always said to me, 'P., the hammers are never very far beneath the surface.' "**

**Paul E. Brown**

**Massillon Quarterback, 1923-25**
**Championship Coach: Massillon Tigers,**
**Ohio State Buckeyes and Cleveland Browns**
**Coach of 14 Championship Teams**
**Founder, Head Coach, GM, Cincinnati Bengals**

*—on Doc Bell's advice when detractors felt that Brown should be fired as Massillon coach in 1933.*

**"One time he cussed at me. I kind of moped and turned around. He** saw how I reacted, so he never cussed me out again. He always encouraged me."

**Mike Byelene**

**All-Ohio Quarterback, Captain, 1936**
**Record-Setting Quarterback, Purdue**

*—on Paul Brown's methods of handling players.*

**"Dave Stewart made me enjoy coaching.** I'd go over to Sharon before I went back to school in the fall and help him out. I was just obsessed with it. I enjoyed it. I was a goner. He recognized this."

*Dave Stewart*

## Paul E. Brown

**Massillon Quarterback, 1923-25**
**Championship Coach: Massillon Tigers, Ohio State Buckeyes and Cleveland Browns**
**Coach of 14 Championship Teams**
**Founder, Head Coach, GM, Cincinnati Bengals**

*—on Dave Stewart, his high school coach at Massillon, who later coached at Sharon, PA.*

**"L.J. Smith was not always in favor of what Paul Brown was doing.** Brown got to be more important than the superintendent of schools. There was some jealousy."

**Pep Paulson**
**First Obie, 1939**
**Booster Club President, 1954**
**Stark County Judge**

*—on Superintendent L.J. Smith's relationship with Paul Brown.*

**"The first I ran into Paul Brown after he got the Massillon job was** down in Lincoln Park. There was a midget league football game. I met him on the sidelines and we walked home together. He was telling me what his plans were. That he was going to copy from **Chic Meehan**, he coached New York University. They were real hot at the time."

**Luther Emery**
**Legendary Massillon Sportswriter**
**Editor of *The Independent***

*—on a conversation with Paul Brown after he was named head coach at Massillon, 1932.*

**"I'll never forget when I got the job at Ohio State, [Doc Bell] always** called me P., P. Brown. He says 'P., you might be wound a little too tight for that kind of a job. I hope you don't explode.' I said, 'I can't think of any better way to go.' That was the sendoff I got from the good doctor."

**Paul E. Brown**

**Massillon Quarterback, 1923-25**
**Championship Coach: Massillon Tigers,**
**Ohio State Buckeyes and Cleveland Browns**
**Coach of 14 Championship Teams**
**Founder, Head Coach, GM, Cincinnati Bengals**

*—on advice from Board of Education President Doc Bell.*

**"One night we lined chairs across the barracks hallway. The coaches** came up and fell all over 'em. **Paul Brown** got us all out of bed. **George Bird** drove the car in front and Brown was in back of us in his car. They ran us five miles. They showed us who was in charge."

**Vernie Weisgarber**

**All-Ohio, 1942**

*—on a training camp stunt that backfired in 1940.*

**"Paul came wandering up and was leaning up against a tree watching** us play football. This was just a neighborhood gang and one of the guys got called to dinner. Paul asked if he could take his place. We finally said O.K. We thought he was too small. He did pretty good then, throwing the ball and so forth. That was my first contact with Paul Brown."

**Luther Emery**

**Legendary Massillon Sportswriter**
**Editor of *The Independent***

*—on his first contact with Paul Brown.*

**"He believed in himself. Most of us have self-doubts, I'm not so sure** he had so many as the general person. He had very good judgment—had it all his life. He could take a situation and analyze it and get it down to what was really important. He could do it succinctly. People always marveled in the NFL meetings. When he would talk, people would pay attention."

**Mike Brown**

**Coach Paul Brown's Son**
**General Manager, Cincinnati Bengals**

*—on his father's self-confidence.*

**"I think we averaged about 150 pounds. We wore equipment, even** shoes, that had been worn before. At the end of that year we played against Canton and elected to go for a dollar a ticket. I can remember being with **Dr. Bell** when we decided this. We did well, we had our little stands, this was down at Edmund Jones field. I think we took in about $2,500, which was good back then. In those days we kept what we made and Canton kept what they made. This gave us a chance to buy uniforms and to start what you know as Massillon football, the way it developed."

**Paul E. Brown**

**Massillon Quarterback, 1923-25**
**Championship Coach: Massillon Tigers, Ohio State Buckeyes and Cleveland Browns**
**Coach of 14 Championship Teams**
**Founder, Head Coach, GM, Cincinnati Bengals**

*—on his first season as coach at Massillon.*

**TIGER TALES**

In nine years at Massillon, Paul Brown recorded 57 shutouts—more than six a season. In both 1934 and 1940, Brown's Tigers racked up nine shutouts in 10 games. Brown, 80-8-2 overall at Massillon, lost only one of his final 60 games.

**"He felt what he was doing at Massillon was important— and you** were sharing it. He was working to make it happen. He wanted to have it turn out the way it should. So you got wrapped up and behind it. The thing he did was get the whole town behind it. Which was a rather extraordinary thing."

**Mike Brown**

**Coach Paul Brown's Son**
**General Manager, Cincinnati Bengals**

*—on his father's accomplishments at Massillon.*

**"I studied the coaches I had. I remember a couple I think I learned as much from because I learned what not to do as what to do."**

**Paul E. Brown**

**Massillon Quarterback, 1923-25**
**Championship Coach: Massillon Tigers, Ohio State Buckeyes and Cleveland Browns**
**Coach of 14 Championship Teams**
**Founder, Head Coach, GM, Cincinnati Bengals**

*—on how he decided to become a football coach.*

# Tiger Swing Band

## SHARING THE EXCELLENCE, TRADITION AND FAME OF THE FOOTBALL - PLAYING TIGERS

Paralleled throughout their history, the Massillon Tiger Swing Band and the Massillon Tiger Football Team are intertwined in excellence.

Both boast legends. **George "Red" Bird,** the famous bandleader; **Paul E. Brown,** the football maestro. Subsequent band directors and football coaches have felt the pressure of living up to the legends.

**Orin "Dykae" Ford** took up the gauntlet from Bird and the Tiger Swing Band didn't miss a beat. As **Chuck Mather** was to Paul Brown, "Dykae" Ford was to George Bird—a legend carrying on a legend.

Today **Chris Smith** walks in legend's shoes. He inspects the spats and makes sure the lines are straight. He understands: Massillon fans expect the best.

**"We had a rehearsal. The kids straggled in. The kids had very** little technique. They were lousy sight readers. We started in and we rehearsed twice a day. Mornings and afternoons. The birth of that band was a hot, sweaty, painful experience. Believe me. The kids would depart at night with bruised and sore lips, sore hands from clappin' rhythm, sore feet from stamping down on the floor trying to maintain a steady beat. I would say to myself, 'I don't think they'll show up tomorrow.' If somebody'd worked me like that I don't know if I would or not. But my golly, the next day they'd come in, their faces shining and bright, and have another go at it."

**George "Red" Bird**

**Band Director, 1938-45**

**Entertainment Director, Cleveland Browns**

**Entertainment Director, Cincinnati Bengals**

*—on the birth of the Massillon Tiger Swing Band, 1938.*

*Scribes said it...*

The orange and black uniformed band triple-timed to the end of the field to a clicking rapid-fire cadence of drumsticks on drum rims. The speed and power-packed show was on.

**DALE MILLER, *AKRON BEACON JOURNAL*, 1967**

*The Massillon Tiger Swing Band, 1942.*

**"The Massillon Band brought the house down at the Ohio State** versus Wisconsin game in 1941. The alums had a meeting the following week and wondered why a high school band could come into that stadium and make the Ohio State Band look so bad. That was the beginning of the Ohio State Band as we know it today."

**Shirley Bird**

**Band Director George "Red" Bird's Daughter**
**Cincinnati Bengals Entertainment Director**

*—on the Massillon Band's first appearance at an Ohio State football game. Massillon legends Paul Brown of Ohio State and Harry Stuhldreher of Wisconsin were the head coaches. George "Red" Bird was the band director.*

**"Words are woefully inadequate to describe the Tiger band. I've seen** the great Trojan band of USC, the swing band of Alabama, Yale and Harvard's fine bands, University of Michigan and our own Ohio State band. Let me say I have never seen a band to equal the Tiger band of Washington High School. It rightfully takes its place as one of the institutions of America. The man responsible should be held up to the high heavens for such a grand job."

**Grant Murray**

**Vice President, Toledo School Board**

*—on Massillon's band and its founder, George "Red" Bird.*

**"The Massillon Band was the first and for years the *only* high** school band that ever appeared at an Ohio State football game."

**Shirley Bird**

**Band Director George "Red" Bird's Daughter**
**Cincinnati Bengals Entertainment Director**

*—on the Massillon Band's reputation at Ohio State.*

*Massillon majorettes in 1940.*

**"Some minister in town wanted to run Red Bird out of town because** the majorettes' skirts were too short. Dad went to [school superintendent] **L.J. Smith** and said, 'Look, I don't want to cause any trouble. I'll just quit. Now you're not going to have to fire me.' Of course they wouldn't let dad quit. Those majorettes are still pretty important in Massillon."

**Shirley Bird**
**Band Director George "Red" Bird's Daughter**
**Cincinnati Bengals Entertainment Director**

*—on a minister's reaction to George "Red" Bird's introduction of "show-business" to halftime shows.*

**"There was a reason behind everything. You might not know** the reason why. And chances are you shouldn't ask him the reason. Just do it. It all seemed to work."

**Shirley Bird**

**Massillon Majorette**
**Band Director George "Red" Bird's Daughter**
**Cincinnati Bengals Entertainment Director**

*—on her father's style as a band director.*

**"The Alma Mater had never been sung before he got there. He** made an arrangement of it and everybody sang the Alma Mater. After five years he decided to shorten it. Newspaper articles said "George Bird is tampering with tradition." He said, 'God, this has only been going on for five years. I'm the one who did it in the first place.' They would *not* let him shorten the Alma Mater."

**Shirley Bird**

**Massillon Majorette**
**Band Director George "Red" Bird's Daughter**
**Cincinnati Bengals Entertainment Director**

*—on Massillon fan's love of the Alma Mater.*

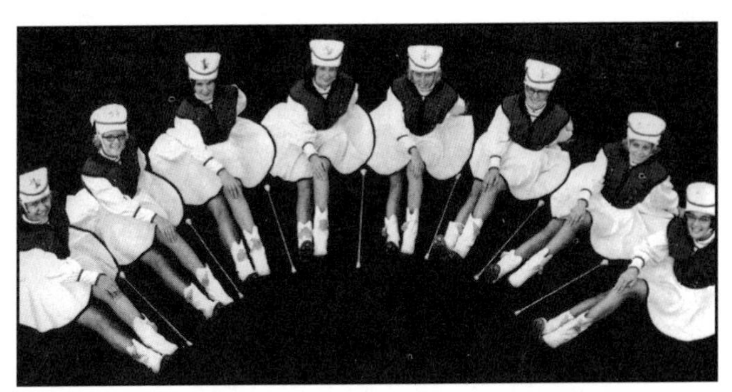

*Massillon's 1965 majorettes: Sumer Domer, Sharon McQueen, Jeanne Nagel, Cheryl Garvin, Jackie Buckland, Linda Yoder, Barb Hoffner and Deborah Belyeat.*

**"He was the first person to ever have majorettes. That was unheard of."**

**Shirley Bird**

**Massillon Majorette**
**Band Director George "Red" Bird's Daughter**
**Cincinnati Bengals Entertainment Director**

*—on her father's idea to use majorettes to front the band.*

**"All of a sudden Doc Luckner [a band member] leaned over on me,** straightened up and threw his horn across the band room. I thought, 'I don't know what he thinks he's doing but this isn't going to go over as a joke.' He dropped dead. And that was probably the most horrible thing we ever experienced. I don't think anybody in the band ever got over that. I can remember going to bed and hearing my father, walking up and down the alley outside our house, sobbing and crying."

**Shirley Bird**

**Massillon Majorette**
**Band Director George "Red" Bird's Daughter**
**Cincinnati Bengals Entertainment Director**

*—on the death of a popular band member.*

**"Paul Brown was a firm believer that when you went to a football** game, you went to be entertained. That was it. It was an entertainment package."

**Shirley Bird**

**Massillon Majorette**
**Band Director George "Red" Bird's Daughter**
**Cincinnati Bengals Entertainment Director**

*—on Paul Brown's philosophy of the total entertainment package.*

**"When I used to come into the band room, written on the blackboard** would be Hitler, Mussolini, Hirohito and Bird for dictators. The little darlings, they just thought the world of me. And they told me."

**George "Red" Bird**

**Massillon Band Director, 1938-45**
**Entertainment Director, Cleveland Browns**
**Entertainment Director, Cincinnati Bengals**

*—on his relationship with the band members.*

**"Paul Brown said, 'I understand you're looking for a band director.** I'll tell you what I have in mind. I'm going places in football. Why can't we have somebody put a good marching band down on the field—put a little entertainment down there and have a good show.' I said, 'I agree with you 100 percent.' As Paul Brown walked out the door I thought of **George Bird**. I wondered where he was."

**L.J. Smith**

**Massillon Superintendent of Schools**

*—on George Bird, a former student of Smith's in Fayette, Ohio, who became Massillon's famed band director.*

**"We used to get ahead and I'd go in and ask the squad if they needed** anything—then I'd go watch the band show. It's nice to be able to do that. I'd tell 'em, I'd just say, 'Well, if everybody's all right, take it easy. I'll be back in a few minutes.' Then I'd go out and watch the band show. I enjoyed the band show, number one. Number two, I knew that they didn't need me. The game was decided."

**Leo Strang**

**Massillon Championship Head Coach, 1958-63**
**State Champs, 1959-61, Nat'l Champs 1959, '61**
**Head Coach, Kent State University**

*—on his enjoyment of the Massillon Band.*

**"They wouldn't give up. I think that's when I realized there's a** different spirit about this town. They wanted to be good. They improved a great deal."

**George "Red" Bird**

**Band Director, 1938-45**
**Entertainment Director, Cleveland Browns**
**Entertainment Director, Cincinnati Bengals**

*—on the birth of the Tiger Swing Band, 1938.*

*Massillon band members always look "just right."*

**"We have an inspection before every performance. We go through, we** check shoes, we check spats, we check gloves. Where's the hat positioned? No hair touching the collar. There's no earrings, there's no nail polish. They take a lot of pride. They take care of those things. It's very seldom to I have to look at a kid and say, 'Hey, you've got earrings in.' They know."

**Chris Smith**

**Massillon Band Director, Since 1991**

*—on the band's tough dress standards.*

**"Our halftime theme was 'Walking Through The Park One Day.' We** got park benches from the city. A landscaper brought in a whole truckload of small trees. We put lights in the trees and made working park lights. They shut out the stadium lights and all at once we lit up the field. The majorettes put on a little dance going through and, the band—they all wore leg lights—marched through the trees and the crowd just went crazy."

**Tom McConnaughy**

**Massillon Industrial Arts Teacher**

*—on an elaborate band show from the 40's.*

**"We're the first high school band in the country to have an apparel** contract. We have shoes, wind suits and t-shirts through Reebok. So when we get off the bus when we travel someplace we all look the same. We go in and rehearse, then we come back to the bus and put our uniforms on. Other bands look at us and say, 'Wow, check them out."

**Chris Smith**

**Massillon Band Director, Since 1991**

*—on the Massillon band's "look."*

*Massillon majorettes lead the band, 1990.*

**"They have to pass a music audition before they can audition** for majorette. They are selected in the spring. They usually attend a one week camp off of our campus. They work all summer with the band. They play in the rehearsals here during the day. They work on their twirling after school. What we're about is music education. If they want to be in the band, they've got to be musicians. A musician who also twirls. They have to pass the music audition. Same with the drum major, same with Obie."

**Chris Smith**

**Massillon Band Director, Since 1991**

*—on the musical standards of Massillon's majorettes.*

**"On Tuesday we do the Touchdown Club luncheon, the Booster Club** rally Tuesday night, Wednesday we have rehearsal and the open house at the high school Wednesday night. Thursday we go play for WHBC radio, we usually go downtown and march around Thursday morning. Then we do the rally on Friday afternoon and the parade Friday night and the game on Saturday."

**Chris Smith**

**Massillon Band Director, Since1991**

*—on the band's hectic McKinley week schedule.*

**"The Booster Club was having a meeting down in the gym and we** had to play for them. We played "Tiger Rag." I never got so sick of a song in my life. But we played "Tiger Rag" for the Booster Club and they thought it was good. The kids thought, hey, this is all right. It was the first time they'd ever gotten a big hand about anything. So that pleased them very much."

**George "Red" Bird**

**Massillon Band Director, 1938-45**
**Entertainment Director, Cleveland Browns**
**Entertainment Director, Cincinnati Bengals**

*—on the Tiger Swing Band's first performance, 1938.*

**"I always felt you were put on this earth to do some good. To have** some sort of an influence or do something to make it a better place than if you hadn't been here. That's my simple philosophy, but that's what I believe."

**George "Red" Bird**

**Band Director, 1938-45**
**Entertainment Director, Cleveland Browns**
**Entertainment Director, Cincinnati Bengals**

*—on the legendary Band Director's credo.*

**"We had a project to write a school song. There was a girl named Helen Chandler**, she played tenor saxophone. She wrote this, and I thought, of all the things that explain the feeling that everyone had for Massillon, this thing that she wrote captured it best. You couldn't put it to march music at all. I'll never forget the words: *In every kick, they'll lay their soul, to put that hide between them poles, and add 'em to their other goals. Yeah Massillon.*"

**George "Red" Bird**

**Band Director, 1938-45**
**Entertainment Director, Cleveland Browns**
**Entertainment Director, Cincinnati Bengals**

*—on a student-written school song for Massillon.*

**"The thing that affects me the most is the Alma Mater. I sit up there in** the stands and about halfway through the Alma Mater I'm bawling like a little baby. That's what we'd have the kids sing out there, they'd sing the Alma Mater."

**Leo Strang**

**Massillon Championship Head Coach, 1958-63**
**State Champs, 1959-61, Nat'l Champs 1959, '61**
**Head Coach, Kent State University**

*—on the Massillon Alma Mater.*

**"For gosh sakes Ken, you're in the band room. You hear what I say.** Why don't you print some of that in the paper. So he did. The next time I saw him he said, 'Bird, don't ever tell me what to write in the paper again. I got more letters from mad people who said that I said bad things about that band. And they told me, that band *can't* be bad.' And so from then on it didn't make any difference what we did out there, every show was greater than the last."

**George "Red" Bird**

**Massillon Band Director, 1938-45**
**Entertainment Director, Cleveland Browns**
**Entertainment Director, Cincinnati Bengals**

*—on newspaper writer Ken Harwick's dilemma.*

**"He was the first one to turn halftime into a *show.* A lot of it was his** show business background. They were all built around a theme. It was also the first theatre in the round on a football field. No matter what part of the field you sat on you could see it."

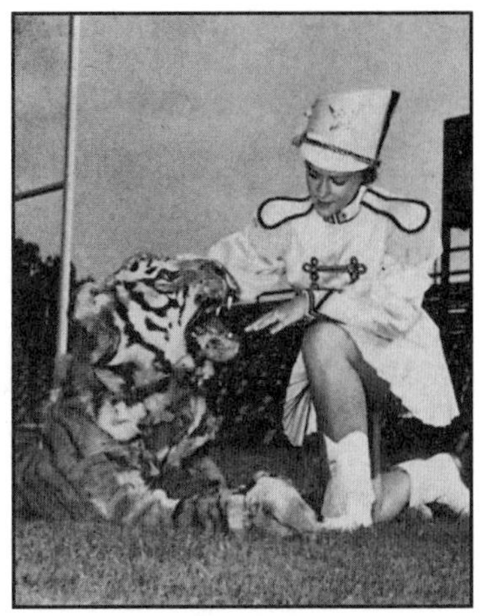

*Obie (Bob Fowler) and majorette Barbara Shipp were part of the show in 1955.*

## Shirley Bird

**Band Director George "Red" Bird's Daughter**
**Cincinnati Bengals Entertainment Director**

*—on some of her father's "firsts."*

*Scribes said it...*

The NBC-TV spotlight was focused on the 92-member Massillon Tiger Swing Band because it was the only high school band east of the Mississippi invited to march in the Tournament of Roses Parade in Pasadena, CA.

***THE YOUNGSTOWN VINDICATOR*, 1955**

**"He said, 'Nothing rhymes with Massillon. Mass-ill-on, Car-ry-on.** That's how he got that. Massillon gave him fits, trying to find something to rhyme with that."

**Shirley Bird**

**Massillon Majorette**
**Band Director George "Red" Bird's Daughter**
**Cincinnati Bengals Entertainment Director**

*—on her father brainstorming for the Massillon standard "Carry On for Massillon."*

**"I got my first baptism of the Tiger band in Erie, Pennsylvania. I never** in my 50 years in sports saw 22,000 people wait after a game to see a high school band perform, and after their school was beaten 74-0, in 1940. Then, weeks later, I saw a crowd sit through a bad rain to see the football game, and then when it was still raining after the game, still sit or stand to see the band again perform. I got a great thrill out of their last song, 'Hold That Tiger.' "

**Grant Murray**

**Vice President, Toledo School Board**

*—on two band shows he witnessed in 1940.*

*The 1939 Massillon Tiger Swing Band.*

**"People were always amazed that Dad's lines were so straight.** Everybody took a 30-inch step, which meant you hit a yard line every five steps. There were red marks all the way down the hallway, every 30 inches, and when you went to the band room you just made sure you hit those marks. It was funny back then, you could always tell band kids because they all walked the same. They all took the same pace."

**Shirley Bird**

**Band Director George "Red" Bird's Daughter**
**Cincinnati Bengals Entertainment Director**

*—on one of "Red" Bird's training methods.*

**"Massillon may have just about the greatest football team in scholastic** ranks throughout the country, but in speaking of its band you can take the word "may" out and be assured that it has the finest; so good, so versatile and inspiring as to be almost unbelievable. When the band came out during the half, the fans cheered like fanatics or were stricken almost dumb by the awe-inspiring sight. As a finale, one that had the crowd stunned, the stadium lights were turned out and the majorettes had lights on the tips of batons while a white Statue of Liberty was illuminated in the center of the field. Fireworks soared into the heavens and the melody of "God Bless America" echoed through the stadium."

**Art Monahan**

**Erie, Pennsylvania, Newspaper Reporter**

*—on the Massillon Swing Band's performance at the 1940 Massillon-Erie East game. Massillon won, 74-0.*

*Scribes said it...*

When you first saw the Massillon Washington High School band strut-run onto the football field, George "Red" Bird was carving a new era in high school band history. His bands left the fans gasping in admiration of their intricately planned halftime show.

**DALE MILLER, *AKRON BEACON JOURNAL,* 1967**

**"George Bird said, 'I'd like to have 64 new musical instruments. Then** I want new uniforms for the band.' I said, 'Take a piece of paper, write out what you want, total it up.' Then I saw the flash. We called a board meeting that night and **Doc Bell**, he was president then, said, 'We've talked long enough. Let's do something, let's act.' He said, 'I make a motion that we employ George and buy him all the equipment that he needs.' We made a motion and they voted unanimously. I thought George was going to fall off the chair. He said, 'Well, it looks like I'm coming to Massillon.'"

*George Bird*

**L.J. Smith**

**Massillon Superintendent of Schools**

*—on the story of George Bird coming to Massillon.*

**"We pull in with our 45-foot moving van. People take notice. The kids like that. They like being special."**

**Chris Smith**

**Massillon Band Director, Since 1991**

*—on one of the perks of being in the Tiger Swing Band.*

**"You knew what you were going to do Monday, you knew what you were going to do Tuesday, you knew you** had a dress rehearsal Wednesday. You knew you could be challenged Thursday. There was an inspection before every ballgame. Just like the military—and God help you if your spats were dirty, your shirt wasn't pressed or your gloves weren't clean. Just *exactly* like you would expect in the military. The kids used to call him Hitler."

**Shirley Bird**

**Massillon Majorette**
**Band Director George "Red" Bird's Daughter**
**Cincinnati Bengals Entertainment Director**

*—on her father's use of military proceedures with the band.*

**"Paul's the one who said the 'Tiger Rag' would be a good tune for the** Massillon Tigers. He had a lot of ideas I used. He was a guy with an imagination."

**George "Red" Bird**

**Band Director, 1938-45**
**Entertainment Director, Cleveland Browns**
**Entertainment Director, Cincinnati Bengals**

*—on Paul Brown's idea to use the old New Orleans standard "Tiger Rag" as Massillon's fight song.*

*Band members in 1939 enjoyed fine instruments and uniforms, thanks to George "Red" Bird—and L.J. Smith.*

**"George Bird said, 'What do you have in the way of instruments to** work with?' I said, 'None. The kids furnish their own.' He said, 'What do you have in the way of uniforms?' I said, 'None. The kids come out in their daily clothes and get what uniforms they can and we do the best we can. Now, are you interested?' "

**L. J. Smith**

**Massillon Superintendent of Schools**

*—on his unusual style of recruiting George Bird.*

**"The fans at Erie wouldn't let the band off the field. They played and** played and I stayed. I finally left to go home and the buses had gone. I saw one come down empty, and I flagged him down. The gang at Watts' confectionary had a little booster club that went to all the ballgames [the 37 Club]. Their bus came by the bus I was in, passed us and pulled up beside us at the traffic light. I was the only passenger on the bus. Somebody yelled, 'Look, the sonofabitch chartered a bus for himself.' "

**Luther Emery**

**Legendary Massillon Sportswriter**
**Editor of *The Independent***

*—on Erie, PA., fans demanding encores from the Massillon Band following Massillon's 74-0 win in Erie, PA., in 1940. The 37 Club often traveled to Cleveland Browns games while Paul Brown coached there. The club was named after the number of seats on the bus they chartered.*

*Scribes said it...*

"And I thought I'd seen everything! I've been to a lot of big college games, I've attended my share of New York stage shows, I've seen plenty of circuses and even a Hollywood premiere, but this thing—well, brother, this thing is different!"

**OUT-OF-TOWN FAN DESCRIBING MASSILLON GAME, *THE EVENING INDEPENDENT*, 1942**

# Booster Club

## POWERFUL, ORGANIZED, EFFECTIVE AND ENDURING

Originated in 1934 to help legendary Head Coach **Paul E. Brown** keep his detractors disarmed, the Massillon Tiger Booster Club has become the benchmark for booster clubs nationwide.

When Brown found public opinion against him following a disappointing loss to Canton McKinley in 1933, Board of Education member **Karl "Kit" Young** conceived the formation of the Booster Club.

Brown, a master of organization, developed the blueprint. He diagramed plays on the chalkboard, explaining his strategies to club members— effectively diffusing potential problems with sound logic. And Massillon fans became football experts.

Today the Booster Club is a marvel of effectiveness. The club accomplishes amazing fund raising projects while carrying on its tradition of support for the coaches and players.

**"There was a movement on, including one board of education** member, to replace Paul Brown after the 1933 McKinley game. We were beaten by Canton McKinley, 21-0. We didn't look good. A lot of Massillon people thought the Tigers should have done better in '33 against McKinley. I think we only gained two first downs. That little movement prompted the organization of the Tiger Booster Club."

**Luther Emery**
**Legendary Massillon Sportswriter**
**Editor of *The Independent***

*—on the events leading to the formation of the Tiger Booster Club in 1934.*

**"Brown stripped the boys down to shorts and had them run** through plays on the gymnasium floor. That's the first time we went public with it."

**Luther Emery**
**Legendary Massillon Sportswriter**
**Editor of *The Independent***

*—on an early Booster Club meeting in Massillon.*

*A packed Booster Club meeting, 1940.*

**"The idea of organizing the Massillon Booster Club was to** help Paul Brown. A member of the Board of Education conceived the idea—his name was **Chick Young**. The purpose was to give Brown an opportunity to talk to the bunch and tell them why such and such happened. Why he did what he did."

**Luther Emery**

**Legendary Massillon Sportswriter**
**Editor of *The Independent***

*—on the birth of the Massillon Booster Club in 1934.*

**"The Booster Club President is responsible for the painting of 1,500 to 2,000 Obie pins. They** have to see that they are painted different than any other Obie pin since 1953. You can get somebody to help—but you have to see that it gets done. It's a chore."

**Junie Studer**

**Massillon Tiger Sign Painter**
**Booster Club President, 1972**

*—on a Booster Club tradition.*

**"If you were an opposing school and you're coming to scout we'd** give you six tickets. We knew where you were sitting and we'd put some loyal boosters right behind you. We'd pick up every comment they made—and they'd report it. Those were behind-the-scenes things that were so important."

**Milan Chovan**

**Massillon Halfback, 1945,**
**Longtime Assistant Coach**

*—on Massillon's scouting tactics.*

**"We figured we needed a project. We were still in the Depression.** Brown figured that some of the players were not getting enough to eat. So we checked 'em. I checked one and the kid had nothing to eat that whole week but potatoes. And it would end up by the end of the week they were boiling the skins and making soup out of the skins. So we decided to give every worthy player a noon lunch at the YMCA. That was our project. I assumed the project by beating the drums in the newspaper."

**Luther Emery**

**Legendary Massillon Sportswriter**
**Editor of *The Independent***

*—on the Booster Club's first project, in 1934.*

**"We were fortunate, Echo Herring, Charlie Anderson and myself, we** ate at the YMCA cafeteria at noon and had milk delivered to the house."

**Mike Byelene**

**All-Ohio, Captain, 1936**
**Record-Setting Quarterback, Purdue**

*—on the Massillon Booster Club's helping hand.*

**"We used to drive kids home after practice. The Tuslaw and Perry** kids would have to stay for football practice, then they wouldn't have a way home. We had a group of boosters that would take turns, every night, driving the country kids home. Most of our big boys were country boys."

**Jim Snively**
**Team Dentist**
**School Board President**

*—on the Booster Club practice of driving the country players home from practice.*

**"I learned in a short time that when you walk into a Booster Club** meeting after you won, you told them why we won—because the players played great. When we lost I told them what I needed to do differently as a coach. Before they could shout it out, I told them myself. Once I started attacking Booster Club meetings like that, they became bearable. In fact I started looking forward to the challenges."

**Lee Owens**
**Massillon Head Coach, 1988-91**
**Head Coach, Akron University**

*—on the challenge of the Booster Club meetings.*

**"I'm amazed at the Booster Club today. These guys raise money.** They raised about $1 million to put that sand turf in. Then they bought all this land that they're developing for a sports complex. To me it's amazing. We're not talkin' little old Massillon coughing up $300 or $400 to feed some kid during the Depression, these guys are bringing in big money."

**Pep Paulson**

**The first Obie, 1939**
**Booster Club President, 1954**
**Stark County Judge**

*—on today's Booster Club.*

**"The Booster Club always said, 'Win or Lose, Massillon Always.' I'm not sure it was going to be 'always' if you lost very much."**

**Tom Harp**

**Massillon Championship Head Coach, 1954-55**
**State Champs, 1954**
**Head Coach Duke, Cornell, Indiana State**
**Assistant to Colonel Blake at Army**

*—on the Booster Club motto.*

**"We had won 20 games in a row and we got beat 19-18 at Warren.** I knew there would be some tough questions at the Booster Club meeting on Monday. So I dressed up with an old slouched hat, dark glasses, a big beard and some sloppy clothes. I just went in and sat down with the rest of the boosters. Nobody recognized me. I could hear people around me saying, 'Where's Strang? I bet he doesn't show up. Well, [assistant coach] **Nick Coso** said, 'Coach Strang put me in charge of gettin' things started tonight.' He showed the movie and then turned the lights on in the auditorium. I get up and start walking down the aisle and take off my fake beard and my glasses. Everybody just started to roar. And that took the edge off of it. I think a lot of them thought I was a little nutsy or something. But that took the edge off and I didn't get those hard questions you often get."

**Leo Strang**

**Massillon Championship Head Coach, 1958-63**
**State Champs, 1959-61, Nat'l Champs 1959, '61**
**Head Coach, Kent State University**

*—on his creative way of dealing with the Booster Club.*

**"A Booster Club member told me there was a big, good-lookin' kid** coming to Massillon. So they arranged for me to be out at the stadium on a Sunday afternoon to meet him and his parents. When he got out of that car, I about flipped. Because here was a handsome guy with a crew cut, 225 pounds, six foot four. You could tell he was an athlete just the way he carried himself. So they came to Massillon. Of course **Bob Vogel** was All-Ohio at Massillon and went on to be All-American and captain at Ohio State and All-Pro with the Baltimore Colts."

**Leo Strang**

**Massillon Championship Head Coach, 1958-63**
**State Champs, 1959-61, Nat'l Champs 1959, '61**
**Head Coach, Kent State University**

*—on his first meeting with Bob Vogel, who moved to Massillon to improve his chances of playing for a major college.*

**"Paul Brown got the tale out that the Booster Club was going to watch us.** If they saw you out late, they were going to report it. They had us stirred up pretty good."

**Edgar "Echo" Herring**

**Massillon's #6 All-Time Scorer (215 points) 1934-36**

*—on the Booster Club's role of community watchdogs.*

**"I was showing a film to the Booster Club one night. The defensive end** hit **Art Hastings**—almost knocked Art down. He went down to one hand, spun around and he had just got straightened out when the linebacker hit him. Then a cornerback hit him. Then another linebacker hit him and the safety hit him. He cut back inside the safety man and went 60 yards for a touchdown. I shut off the projector and I told the Booster Club, 'Gentlemen, I'm gonna tell you something about that play. That's great coaching.' "

**Leo Strang**

**Massillon Championship Head Coach, 1958-63**
**State Champs, 1959-61, Nat'l Champs 1959, '61**
**Head Coach, Kent State University**

*—on elusive Art Hastings, Massillon's all-time leading rusher (3,090).*

# The Players

## WITHOUT THEM, THERE WOULD BE NO MASSILLON FOOTBALL

Who is the most important person in Massillon football? An old sage might say, "**Paul Brown**, the father of modern football." Others may say, "It has to be the head coach." Many come to mind from throughout the glorious history of Massillon Tiger football.

Massillon Tiger football experts—and there are a lot of them—could debate the question into the wee hours of the morning. There are so many names. **Paul Brown, Luther Emery, L. J. Smith, Doc Bell, Chuck Mather, Earle Bruce, Don James, Horace Gillom, Ace Crable, Chris Spielman**—the list goes on and on.

Like so many questions, the answer is obvious, yet so often overlooked. Of course it's the player who is most important. Whether that player is a star or the last player off the bench.

**"We're in the coaches' room and I hear this noise starting out in the** locker room. It's a rumble, it's a roar, it's a pounding, screaming, it's a growling. I said, 'What the hell's the matter out there?' They said, 'That's just the way they are before a game.' I said, 'What do you mean?' They said, 'They're just getting themselves ready to play football.' I stuck my head in the locker room. I mean these guys are beatin' on each other, growlin', they're screamin', they're getting themselves fired up. I said, 'So much for a pep talk. They don't need any pep talk tonight. Don't get 'em calmed down so they can hear what I have to say. Just turn 'em loose.' "

**Tom Harp**

**Massillon Championship Head Coach, 1954-55**
**State Champs, 1954**
**Head Coach Duke, Cornell, Indiana State**
**Assistant to Colonel Blake at Army**

*—on his first game as Massillon's head coach.*

*Scribes said it...*

An estimated 2,500 persons last night stood in line as long as five hours awaiting an opportunity to buy tickets to the Massillon-Canton McKinley football game. Starting at Rider's drug store, the line snaked its way four persons long for over four blocks.

***THE AKRON BEACON JOURNAL*, 1940**

**"Al Brown was a real strong leader vocally, but mainly he was our** number one back. You hear about **Ace Crable**, you hear about **Clarence Johnson**, you hear about **Dick Jacobs.** But the back on that football team was Al Brown. He made all the touchdowns—he was a great running back. The *moves*—of course he played first team as a sophomore. He was a real street fighter. There wasn't a guy on that football team that wanted to take Al Brown on. He had a reputation from junior high school. He was tougher than hell. For a guy who wasn't that big, he'd take anybody on."

*Al Brown*

**Jack Hill**

**Massillon Quarterback, 1946-48**
**Booster Club President, 1967**

*—on Captain Al Brown, who at 5'7", 152, commanded respect.*

**"I refused to shine shoes because I played first team, too. Sophomores** had to shine the upper classmen's shoes. Well, I didn't polish no shoes. I was the type of guy, if you want to get it on, well, we'd get it on. I never had to shine shoes."

**Hase McKey**
**2-Time 1st Team All-Ohio, 1958-59**
**Arizona State Star**

*—on avoiding the sophomore shoe-shining duty.*

**"In Massillon, growing up, everybody knew you from what you did on the football field. You** were standing out. That's what you played for. To be recognized. If your name's on that jersey, you're getting credit for what you did. Somebody's lookin'. Leo Strang had the right idea."

**David Whitfield**
**All-Ohio 1965**
**Captain, Ohio State, 1970**

*—on new coach Earle Bruce's decision to remove the names from the players' jerseys.*

Homer Floyd

**"Homer Floyd looked like a thoroughbred.** He just bounced when he walked—it was like twinkletoes or something. Nice looking, streamlined kid. Didn't weigh much, 155 pounds. Could run like the wind, cut on a dime."

## Tom Harp

**Massillon Championship Head Coach, 1954-55**
**State Champs, 1954**
**Head Coach Duke, Cornell, Indiana State**
**Assistant to Colonel Blake at Army**

*—on Homer Floyd, fifth all-time leading rusher (2,370).*

*Scribes said it...*

The Massillon citizen-school cooperation, for a city of 29,000, it probably produces the most colorful football program in the country. You might call it professionalism..I don't..I call it a matter of "doing things right."

**ALLAN WHITE, LIMA NEWS, 1953**

**"The excitement of the big attendance. We always heard that** Massillon outdrew 90 percent of the colleges. You grew up with that. That's kind of what you expected. It was really a thrill to be a part of that and play."

**Don James**

**Massillon Championship Quarterback, 1949**
**Record-Breaking Quarterback, Univ. of Miami**
**National Championship Coach,**
**University of Washington, 1991**

*—on the thrill of playing at Massillon.*

**"Us boys, there were four of us slept in one bed. Three long ways** and one at the foot. The littlest one slept at the foot. But we managed. We had a close family relationship there."

**Howard Houston**

**Massillon Jeweler**
**One of Massillon's famous Houston Brothers**

*—on his family's life on a Southern Illinois farm, prior to their move to Massillon.*

**"They were playing in Lincoln Park—we used** to call it The Bottoms—I didn't know Dave Canary from anybody else. But I saw this little fella stoppin' the end runs. I said, 'Who is that?' Someone said, 'That's Dave Canary.' He was a little hard-nose player."

**Luther Emery**

**Massillon Sportswriter**
**Editor of *The Independent***

*David Canary*

*—on his first memory of David Canary, All-Ohio at Massillon, All-American at Cincinnati.*

**"The only position he could play was, just stick him in front of the center and say 'Sic 'em.' "**

**Leo Strang**

**Massillon Championship Head Coach, 1958-63**
**State Champs, 1959-61, Nat'l Champs 1959, '61**
**Head Coach, Kent State University**

*—on Lawson White: Wrestler and All-Ohio nose guard.*

**"They'd say, 'You're too small to play middle guard.' No, there was** no way I would believe that. I had just watched my brothers do this. Then there were guys like **Ducky Schroeder** who said, 'Your brother was a guard and you're going to be a guard.' Ducky knew that he could teach you the technique—as long as you had heart. That was the thing he was concerned about. And the Whitfields always had the heart."

**David Whitfield**
**All-Ohio 1965**
**Captain, Ohio State, 1970**

*—on his ability to play on the line despite a lack of size.*

**"I asked the Ohio State coaches, 'How can you play a guy that small** at defensive end?' They said, 'If we had *all* **Dave Whitfields**, we'd win every football game. He doesn't know what it is to loaf. He plays with intensity every play of every game."

**Carl "Ducky" Schroeder**
**Legendary Massillon Assistant, 1948-70**
**Massillon Player, 1923**

*—on David Whitfield, Massillon All-Ohio, Ohio State Captain, who played at 170 pounds.*

**"Our Sunday school teacher told us the world was going to end. I said a prayer to God, 'Please don't let it end until I get to play for Massillon.' I was about 8 or 9 years old."**

*Steve Luke*

**Steve Luke**
**All-Ohio, 1970**
**Three time Rose Bowl Starter**
**Ohio State University, 1972-74**
**Green Bay Packers Captain**

*—on a young Massillon boy's prayer.*

**TIGER TALES**

"We sold out for the 100th Massillon-McKinley game in an hour and a half. People started lining up at 4 a.m. Tickets went on sale at 7:30. The newspaper took pictures of people fanning out their tickets and put it on the front page. People complained about that for three weeks because they thought we were selling more than two tickets per person."

**MICHELLE WOLFE, TICKET MANAGER, 1998**

**"I think every kid who puts on that uniform at Massillon is great. Some** kids are a little faster, a little quicker, a little stronger. But every kid who puts on that uniform has a heart of gold. That's one thing about the Massillon kids that you can't take away from them—that other schools don't have—our kids have that tradition. They're out there for a reason."

**Nick Vrotsos**

**Legendary Massillon Assistant, 1958-84**

*—on Massillon players.*

**"The Houston family was a remarkable football family. Lindell, Jack** [Purdue captain], **Walt** and **Jim** [Ohio State Captain] all played college football. Lindell and Jim made All-American. They were all good football players. All of them. They weren't cocky. Just down to earth fellas. They always said that their brother **Howard** would have been the best of all. He lost his legs in an auto accident. They were all good boys."

**Luther Emery**

**Legendary Massillon Sportswriter**

**Editor of *The Independent***

*—on Massillon's famous Houston brothers.*

**"I've always thought that Dennis Franklin was the best quarterback that Massillon has ever had. I always** thought that Dennis was just a special player. He had the class and finesse of a Joe Namath. To me, Dennis Franklin epitomized the position of quarterback. He was cocky, he was confident, he was classy."

*Dennis Franklin*

**Steve Luke**

**All-Ohio, 1970**
**Three-Time Rose Bowl Starter**
**Ohio State University, 1972-74**
**Green Bay Packers Captain**

*—on Massillon and Michigan star Dennis Franklin.*

**TIGER TALES**

**MASSILLON PLAYS BEFORE 187,500 FANS IN 10-GAME SCHEDULE**

The Massillon Tigers played before 187,500 during the 1945 season, breaking their own single season attendance record of 180,500, set in 1940.

**"Homer Floyd had an amazing, relaxed change of pace about him** that made him incredibly, deceptively hard to tackle. He'd give that *hooph,* and I'd see him swing into that gear where he'd sink a little lower and almost stop and then *pfft,* he's gone. I saw people missing him for a couple of years. I felt sorry for them."

**David Canary**
**All-Ohio, 1956**
**All-American, University of Cincinnati, 1959**
**4-Time Emmy Winner, "All My Children**
**""Candy" on "Bonanza"**

*—on All-Ohio running back Homer Floyd, Massillon's #5 all-time leading rusher.*

**"I always liked the shiftiness of Irvin Crable, but I could never do it. He** could reverse field, make you miss, cut on a dime. I don't think I tried to run like any certain player, but I admired a lot of them."

**Homer Floyd**
**Legendary Massillon running back, 1952-54**
**All-Ohio, 1954**
**University of Kansas star, 1955-58**

*—on one of his childhood heroes.*

**"I told Eddie, 'If you make good at Massillon I'll write to Elmer Layden**

*Eddie Molinski*

at Notre Dame and recommend you.' I didn't hear a word from Eddie from then on, until the practice the Friday night before the game with Canton McKinley. Eddie saw me standing on the sidelines and came over and said, 'You know you told my family if I made good you'd write a letter to Notre Dame.' I said, 'Yes, I remember that.' He said, 'Well, do you think I made good?' I said, 'I think you did, now I'll write the letter.' Layden wrote back and said he'd send some alumni. Sure enough some alumni came down and talked to him, but they didn't come to any kind of an agreement. Eddie looked all around and finally landed at Tennessee, where he was All-American."

**Luther Emery**

**Legendary Massillon Sportswriter**
**Editor of *The Independent***

*—on his promise to Eddie Molinski.*

**"Players coming out of Massillon's winning program know what they're doing. They're highly competitive. They're used to winning.**

**Bo Schembechler**

**Legendary Michigan Head Coach**
**Ohio State Assistant Coach**

*—on qualities he's seen in Massillon's football players.*

**"Massillon kids believe that they should win and that they will win.** They're raised that way. When you have that confidence it can be a big advantage for you."

**Chris Spielman**

**Massillon: 2-time All-Ohioan, All-American,**
**USA Today Defensive Player of the Year, 1983**
**Ohio State: 2-time All-American,**
**Lombardi Award Winner**
**NFL: Detroit Lions, Buffalo Bills, Since 1988**
**Four Pro Bowls**

*—on the attitude of Massillon players.*

**"Bob Glass, I'll grant you, broke every rule that Paul Brown ever** made. I saw him smoke, drink beer. But he was just a fun-loving guy who didn't give a shit. He was one of those 'Go to Hell' guys who loved to have a helluva good time. But he could play football. Had that been a lesser player, Brown would have had him out of there a long time ago."

*Bob Glass*

**Earl "Ick" Martin**

**Captain, All-Ohio Center**
**1939 State Championship Team**

*—on Bob Glass, Massillon's all-time leading scorer, 1935-37 (331 points).*

**"I don't think there's ever been a greater fullback than Bob Glass."**

**Edgar "Echo" Herring**

**Massillon's #6 All-Time Scorer (215 points)**
**1934-36**

*—on Bob Glass, 1935-37.*

**"To start as a sophomore, you had to be good and you had to be** lucky. You had to be an outstanding player. And you had to be lucky in that you better not have an All-Ohio ahead of you in that position."

**Dale Walterhouse**

**Longtime Massillon Assistant**

*—on starting as a sophomore at Massillon.*

**"People said that I couldn't start as a sophomore at Massillon. I just** felt like that didn't have anything to do with me. I just thought that I'd be starting. It turned out things worked out for me."

**Chris Spielman**

**Massillon: 2-time All-Ohioan, All-American,**
**USA Today Defensive Player of the Year, 1983**
**Ohio State: 2-time All-American,**
**Lombardi Award Winner**
**NFL: Detroit Lions, Buffalo Bills, Since 1988**
**Four Pro Bowls**

*—on becoming a rare sophomore starter at Massillon.*

**"This kid, my dad got him to go to college. His dad was an immigrant,**

he worked on the railroad. He was angry about this. He was going to do some damage to my father for having his kid go to college. Because he thought his son should work on the railroad. His mother brought my mother a pillowcase she embroidered and my mother cherished that. She kept that for many, many years."

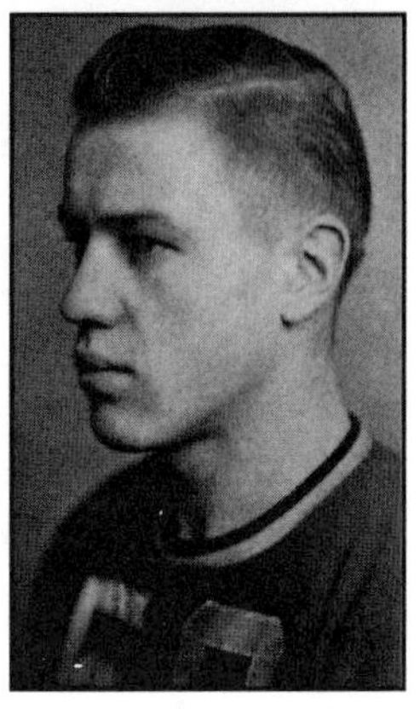

*Mike Byelene*

**Mike Brown**

**Coach Paul Brown's Son**
**General Manager, Cincinnati Bengals**

*—on Mike Byelene, Paul Brown's quarterback at Massillon (1934-36). Mike Brown was named after Byelene.*

**"Reichenbach and I could work the blocking sled like a team of horses.**

We hit that thing a lot. We could drive that baby 15 yards. We were good because we were a team."

**Jim Schumacher**

**Massillon Tackle, 1948-50**
**Ohio State Tackle**

*—on the teamwork between he and Jim Reichenbach.*

**"I was home from the service and George Slusser had joined the Air** Corps. I stopped over to see his mother. She was so worried about him. I told her, 'Mrs. Slusser, they lose more pilots in flight training than in combat.' I was trying to make her feel better. Two days before the damn war's over he got shot down. After that happened I couldn't face her. They never found him. He was just lost in the Pacific. He was a good-looking kid. He had all the girls after him. Anybody that would meet George would have liked him."

**Earl "Ick" Martin**

**Captain, All-Ohio Center**
**1939 State Championship Team**

*—on George Slusser, All-Ohio Quarterback (1939), Ohio State star and WWII pilot.*

*Scribes said it...*

The Cathedral Latins, scholastic champs of our town, have a deep and painful appreciation today of why Massillon is the daffiest high school football town in these gridiron ga-ga United States. The Latins, unbeaten in 17 previous starts, got romped over last night by the Massillon Tigers, 40-13.

**BEN WILLIAMSON**
***CLEVELAND PLAIN DEALER,* 1939**

**"I enjoyed seeing my son play, doing something I did."**

*Willie Spencer, Jr.*

## Willie Spencer, Sr.

**All-Ohio running back, 1971**
**World Football League Star, 1974-75, Memphis**
**NFL running back: Minnesota Vikings, Washington Redskins, New York Giants**

*—on seeing his son, Willie, Jr., win All-Ohio quarterback honors in 1994. They are the only father and son combination to win first team All-Ohio honors at Massillon.*

*Scribes said it...*

The Vikings and nine other NFL teams are very much interested in Willie Spencer, who is, beyond question, the most-sought player from the WFL. Spencer is cast as "bigger, stronger, faster and a better blocker than **Larry Csonka.**"

**RALPH REEVES, *ST. PAUL PIONEER PRESS,* 1975**

**“Roger Price said, ‘Jim, we can’t use you, you’re wasting your time.** Why don’t you wait until next year to come out.’ I tried out in seventh grade. He cut me. I was so devastated about that. I had a very, very bad, sick feeling. The world came down around me. What would my parents say? What would my brothers say? What would my friends say? This good for nothing kid got cut. It made me wonder how I could get through life without being a member of the team. Being a part of that wonderful organization. I wanted to make my mom and dad proud. I went home and talked to my mom about that. She said, ‘Don’t worry about it, try next year.’ That’s what my brothers said, too. I tried out in eighth grade and made it. Came to the ninth grade I had grown quite a bit. I had the determination, I guess. Roger Price had proven me to be a failure. It was kind of a reverse psychology thing, you put a kid down and he’ll fight back harder every time. I was determined I’d never get cut again.”

**Jim Houston**

**Massillon: All-Ohio, 1955**
**Ohio State: All-American, 1958-59**
**Cleveland Browns: Four Pro Bowls**

*—on the devastation of being cut. His brother Lin was playing with the Cleveland Browns and brothers Jack and Walt were playing for the Tigers at the time.*

**"In practice no one could block Billy Wallace. Couldn't keep him** out. Earl Martin hook-blocked him right in the face. He was bleedin' and everything. About knocked him out. He had to hook block to get him. No one could block him."

*Bill Wallace*

## Ray Getz

**All-Ohio, 1939, Co-Captain, 1940**

*—on 5'6", 149 pound All-Ohio guard Bill Wallace. Massillon opponents couldn't block Wallace, either.*

**"When Harry Stuhldreher was at Notre Dame, the Tigers would start** their summer practice before Notre Dame. 'Stuhlie' would come down and work out with the Massillon team."

## Luther Emery

**Legendary Massillon Sportswriter**
**Editor of *The Independent***

*—on former Tiger quarterback Harry Stuhldreher practicing with Massillon while he was quarterback of the famed "Four Horsemen of Notre Dame."*

**"Being on the Wheaties box was great—but it was also very difficult** for a 17-year-old kid. Over night I became a role model for a lot of kids. It was the first time I had people start staring at me, recognizing me. It made me feel funny. I became very self-consious. You feel like you have to live up to this standard. I was just trying to hang out with my buddies. I was visiting sick kids in the hospital. And that was great. If I could make a kid who was sick feel better, or get better, I certainly didn't mind doing that. But at 17, I wasn't prepared for it. Every time I was in public I felt like I had to live up to "the boy that was on the Wheaties box." I was afraid to be myself. I learned, I grew up fast. I think I was a good kid. I did a lot of good things. I never could say no. I wanted to do the right thing. It was great, but it was very difficult for a 17-year-old kid to do."

**Chris Spielman**

**Massillon: 2-time All-Ohioan, All-American,**
**USA Today Defensive Player of the Year, 1983**
**Ohio State: 2-time All-American,**
**Lombardi Award Winner**
**NFL: Detroit Lions, Buffalo Bills, Since 1988**
**Four Pro Bowls**

*—on the psychological pressure of being on the Wheaties box as a high school student.*

## "[Coach]Lee Tressel cut me the week before the McKinley game.

*Ivory Benjamin*

It was after the Barberton game, the night I was named High School All-American. I wanted to hurry up and get home. I rode home with the wrong people. He was worried. Because he's responsible for me. Monday morning he tells me I'm *done.* I'm sick. I'm cryin'. I'm a big shot, but I'm cryin'. And I beg and I beg. Because I I wanted to play in the McKinley game. He let me come back, but he let me know who the boss was."

**Ivory Benjamin**

**Legendary Massillon running back, 1955-57**
**All-American, All-Ohio,**
**Stark County MVP, 1957**

*—on being disciplined by Head Coach Lee Tressel.*

*Scribes said it...*

In the Tiger dressing room hangs a sign that reads something like this: "The team that gets the first six inches wins the ball game."

**LUTHER EMERY**
***THE EVENING INDEPENDENT*, 1940**

**"Joe Sparma was a pure passer. Just an outstanding pure pro** passer. That's the reason I wanted him to go to school where he could pocket pass. But **Woody Hayes** was a hell of a salesman. Woody didn't want him to go to a school in the Big 10 and pass against him. I don't think there's any doubt about it that Sparma could have been a great pro football player."

**Leo Strang**

**Massillon Championship Head Coach, 1958-63**
**State Champs, 1959-61, Nat'l Champs 1959, '61**
**Head Coach, Kent State University**

*—on All-Ohio quarterback Joe Sparma's decision to go to Ohio State instead of Michigan State.*

**"A guy who was tough was that safety man, John Frieg. His dad owned Frieg's restaurant downtown. He hit your ass."**

**Earle Bruce**

**Championship Coach, 1964-65**
**State Champs, #2 in Nation, 1964-65**
**Head Coach, Ohio State University**

*—on the son of Frieg's restaurant owner Gene "Spider" Frieg. Frieg's was a local landmark.*

**"Goose Gatsios was an ass-kicker. Nobody messed with him. And when I said nobody, I mean nooo-body. He wasn't a** big guy, but he wasn't scared. Goose used to run behind me when he played quarterback. He was a great runner."

*"Goose" Gatsios*

## "Big" Ben Bradley

**All-American, All-Ohio Center, 1962**

*—on 5'8", 153-pound quarterback and defensive back Thomas "Goose" Gatsios (1962-63).*

**"They were having a scrimmage and Tommy got away for a pretty** good run. I thought he was too small. I said to Paul [Brown], 'Who is that little fella there?' He said, 'Tommy James. He's gonna be a good one.' "

## Luther Emery

**Legendary Massillon Sportswriter**
**Editor of *The Independent***

*—on his first memory of Tommy James—Massillon, Ohio State and Cleveland Browns star.*

**"Those Wallace boys were some kids. One time, it was raining after** practice. So finally I told Bobby and Barney, 'I'll drive you on home.' It was really wet. Their mother came out and said, 'What are you trying to do, spoil these boys? They can walk home in the rain.' She was a tough old gal. She was just a little woman, but she was tough. They were tough kids. But nice kids."

**Bud Houghton**

**Championship Head Coach, 1941, 1946-47**
**State Champs, 1941**
**Massillon player, 1925-26**

*—on brothers Bill, Barney and Bob Wallace. Bill was an All-Ohio guard in 1940; Bob was an All-Ohio running back in 1943. Barney started at center but was drafted into World War II missing his senior year and his chance at All-Ohio honors.*

## "Running from the Police"

**Irvin "Ace" Crable**

**Legendary Massillon Running Back**
**All-Ohio, Stark County Player of the Year, 1949**

*—on how he developed his elusive moves.*

*David Canary, 1954.*

**"Dave Canary was the toughest, hardest-** nosed kid I ever coached. One night he blocked an extra point against Mansfield that preserved a 12-12 tie. He blocked it with his face. He ruptured a blood vessel in his eye and his eye was shut. He just kept right on going. He was solid as a rock and tough. Intelligent. He knew what he wanted to do. He wanted to go to the University of Cincinnati and study dramatics."

## Tom Harp

**Massillon Championship Head Coach, 1954-55**
**State Champs, 1954**
**Head Coach Duke, Cornell, Indiana State**
**Assistant to Colonel Blake at Army**

*—on All-Ohio, All-American and actor David Canary.*

**"Massillon kids weren't that big. Dick Whitfield was a good example** of that. He was not very big. He was just fast and quick and strong—and he came after ya."

**Mike Hershberger**

**All-Ohio, Captain, 1956**

**Major League Baseball Player, 1961-71**

*—on Dick Whitfield, oldest of five Whitfield brothers at Massillon. Brothers Dick (1956), David (1965) and George (1968) were all Tiger captains.*

**"You had to do what they did. They were part of the team out** training you in the streets. If you got hurt or fell down, you better not cry. Because big brother was watching you. Big brother also taught you how to play football. The proper stance. The proper way to fire out. Those things were passed down. Richard passed that down to Charlie. Charlie passed it down to Tom and I. My brothers were the best coaches I ever had."

**David Whitfield**

**All-Ohio 1965**

**Captain, Ohio State, 1970**

*—on the profound influence of his brothers.*

## "I had a legend stop by to see me when I was in junior high: Paul "Bear" Bryant. I was in class and they came up and got me.

*Bill Harmon*

It was the time of year he was on a recruiting trip. He was in the area and stopped by to see me. He had his plaid hat on and everything. They kind of just look you over, that's what they're doing. Just casual conversation. He said, 'I just wanted to stop by and meet ya.' I was real honored to meet him. I was just an eighth-grader then. I later took a trip down there. I visited him. I went right in his big crimson office. He had that deep southern drawl—it was kind of hard to understand."

**"Big" Bill Harmon**

**All-Ohio Fullback, 1975**

**#4 All-time rushing leader**

*—on being recruited by legendary Alabama coach Paul "Bear" Bryant. Bryant spoke at the Massillon football banquet in 1951.*

**"Myself, I was headed in the same direction as my brothers, but I got** run over by a truck. I lost both of my legs at that time. I loved the game. I played it hard. I guess I was pretty good at it. I played quarterback at Jones Junior High. I could outrun my brother Lin in the 100-yard dash when he was in college and I was in eighth grade. You never know how it would have turned out. I just feel great gratitude that maybe this accident was for a purpose. God was good enough to me to let me live and maybe that was how He had it planned. I don't know any other reason. That's the way life is, I guess."

**Howard Houston**

**One of Massillon's famous Houston Brothers**

*—on the accident that changed his life. His brothers Lin, Jim and Walter played professional football.*

**"I got hit pretty hard and had to come out of the game. Coach Strang said,** 'Hase, Hase, come here. I want you to go in there and get *vicious*.' I still hadn't come back to my senses, I said, 'What's his number, what's his number?' "

**Hase McKey**

**2-time 1st Team All-Ohio, 1958-59**

**Arizona State Star**

*—on a humorous incident with head coach Leo Strang.*

**"Bob Vogel was a master technician at offensive tackle. Beautiful technique, quick feet."**

*Bob Vogel*

**Bo Schembechler**

**Legendary Michigan Head Coach**
**Ohio State Assistant Coach**

*—on Massillon's Bob Vogel was an All American and Captain at Ohio State (1962).*

**"Johnny Traylor would sometimes get hit hard, his helmet would be** all twisted on his head, but he'd still get up and keep coming back. Sometimes you could see the water welling up in his eyes. Then he'd get the ball again and come right back at ya."

**Homer Floyd**

**Legendary Massillon Running Back, 1952-54,**
**All-Ohio, 1954**
**University of Kansas Star, 1955-58**

*—on All-Ohio(1953) running back Johnny Traylor.*

**"I felt 'I can't be tested at a higher level, at this age, than I am right** now.' And I was able to perform like I did as a sophomore. That's when I knew I belonged as a starter at Massillon. I had just played the best team in the country and held my own."

**Chris Spielman**

**Massillon: 2-time All-Ohioan, All-American,**
**USA Today Defensive Player of the Year, 1983**
**Ohio State: 2-time All-American,**
**Lombardi Award Winner**
**NFL: Detroit Lions, Buffalo Bills, Since 1988**
**Four Pro Bowls**

*—on his performance against Cincinnati Moeller, at the Akron Rubber Bowl in 1981. Massillon lost, 24-6.*

**"I had profound respect for their accomplishments in Massillon and** the precision of Paul Brown's teams at Massillon. I really looked up to those guys."

**Ara Parseghian**

**Championship Head Coach, Notre Dame**

*—on Tiger stars Lin Houston, Tommy James and Horace Gillom. He later played with the three players with the Cleveland Browns.*

**"Edgar Herring. Paul Brown called him 'Echo' because he was real fast. He'd say, 'Here he comes, there he goes.' He was just an echo."**

**Augie Morningstar**
**All-Ohio, Captain, 1935**
**Head Coach, Massillon, 1945**
**Championship Head Coach, Mansfield, 1949**

*Edgar Herring*

*—on speedy running back Edgar "Echo" Herring (1934 -36), Massillon's #6 all-time scorer (215 points).*

**"My father always said, 'It's cheaper to move than to pay rent.' We moved 17 times."**

**Howard Houston**
**Massillon Jeweler**
**One of Massillon's famous Houston Brothers**

*—on his father's propensity to move.*

**"I don't think anybody's ever had a better pair of ends on a high school** football team. **Jim Houston** was All-American at Ohio State and a famous Cleveland Brown. **Dave Canary** was All-American at Cincinnati. Even though today Dave's an actor in Hollywood, every coach he's ever played for told me he was the hardest hitter they ever saw. He's a great guy to have on a football team. The two of them were not only great football players, they were great people. I don't think it took too much coaching with them. I could think up jokes to tell on the banquet circuit while I was coaching those two."

**Carl "Ducky" Schroeder**

**Legendary Massillon Assistant, 1948-70**

**Massillon Player, 1923**

*—on two of his top ends at Massillon, 1954-55.*

**"You hear the crack of the pads. You wonder, 'Am I going to be able to** stand up to this?' This is a different phase all together. In junior high you hear a little crack and pop. But you don't hear pads cracking. That was the big impression—the crack of the pads."

**Lee Nussbaum**

**All-Ohio Running Back, 1952**

*—on his first impression of varsity football at Massillon.*

**"You talk about a great player from Massillon—Jim Houston's the guy.** He was a beautiful blocker. He was a great defensive end. He played great both ways."

*Jim Houston*

**Bo Schembechler**

**Legendary Michigan Head Coach**
**Ohio State Assistant Coach**

*—on Massillon's Jim Houston who was All-Ohio(1955) at Massillon and a two time All-American(1958-59) and Captain (1959) at Ohio State.*

**"I'd say, you take this cat, I'll take this cat. They wouldn't believe us,** but that's the way we'd do it when they threw some funny kind of defense at us. We called it cat blocking."

**Hase McKey**

**2-Time 1st Team All-Ohio, 1958-59**
**Arizona State Star**

*—on a blocking scheme he and Jim Houston used.*

**"Joe Sparma had a Bonneville, we got a flat tire, the jack slipped and** it was falling. They said, 'It's fallin', it's fallin'.' I rammed my shoulder into the side of the fender. It was enough to push it back over. They bragged and said, 'Hase held that car up.' I just steadied it."

**Hase McKey**

**2-Time 1st Team All-Ohio, 1958-59**

**Arizona State Star**

*—on an incident en route to a players-only summer practice at Joe Sparma's father's farm.*

**"At halftime Rick Spielman said, 'Coach, help me get these pads on my hands'—his hands were** shaking, I said, 'Rick, what's the matter?' He said, 'My thumbs are hurting. Just help me get my pads on and I'll be alright.' I talked to the trainer, I said, 'take a look at his hands, what do you think?' The trainer said his thumbs were broken. He had played that way for awhile. I said, Rick, you can't play that way.' He said, 'Just help me get the pads back on, I can play.' "

**Dale Walterhouse**

**Longtime Assistant Coach**

*—on a player's desire: State Championship game, 1980.*

**"Stanfield Wells was Massillon's first All-American. He was a fine man,** big fellow, played a little pro ball. I went up to Michigan to meet him. He was overjoyed. He got to talking and asking about some of the Massillon people he graduated with. He went back in his bedroom and came out with his Massillonian in his hand. He asked me about quite a number of ones who were in there."

*Stanfield Wells*
(Photo courtesy University of Michigan Photo Archives)

**Luther Emery**
**Legendary Massillon Sportswriter**
**Editor of *The Independent***

*—on the star of the 1906 Tigers, who, according to the 1907 Massillon yearbook, "circled the end for most of Massillon's gains last football season, thus winning glory and the affections of a charming sophomore." Wells was All-American at Michigan (1910).*

**"Harry Stuhldreher talked to me, I didn't talk to him. He said I was** too small. But he was smaller than me and played for Notre Dame."

**Mike Byelene**

**All-Ohio, Captain, 1936**
**Record-Setting quarterback, Purdue**

*—on Wisconsin Head Coach Harry Stuhldreher, a former Massillon quarterback, who rejected Byelene after a recruiting visit.. Byelene starred for Purdue, throwing a 16-yard touchdown pass and running 73 yards for another score to beat Stuhldreher's Wisconsin team.*

**"Heine's only problem, he and Brown didn't get along too well.** Some of the guys would sneak around and smoke. Heine was one of 'em. He'd get him out there sometimes before practice and run him, because he knew he smoked. He'd make him pay for it. Sometimes he'd be out there vomiting, he run him so much—tryin' to break him from that habit."

**Edgar "Echo" Herring**

**Massillon's #6 all-time scorer (215 points) 1934-'36**

*—on Paul Brown disciplining star runner Heine Krier.*

**Everybody recognizes you. You walk in school and people look at you and admire you. It** was great. I thought, 'I know how a movie star feels now.' People treat you real nice. The principal lets you get away with little stuff they don't let other people get away with. I enjoyed it."

*Tom Hannon*

**Tom Hannon**
**All-Ohio, 1972**
**2-Time All-Big 10,**
**Michigan State, 1975-76**
**Minnesota Vikings Star, 1977-83**

*—on life as the star player at Massillon.*

**"He said, 'Live the way I expect you to live. Clean. Don't insult people.' "**

**Augie Morningstar**
**All-Ohio, Captain, 1935**
**Head Coach, Massillon, 1945**
**Championship Head Coach, Mansfield, 1949**

*—on Paul Brown's instructions to his 1935 captain.*

**"Horace Gillom could put the ball out of sight as a punter. He still** would be great in today's game. He would put that thing up there and it would just soar. He could kick it up high above the lights and turn it over."

**Ara Parseghian**

**Championship Head Coach, Notre Dame**

*—on watching Massillon's Horace Gillom punt in high school and with the Cleveland Browns.*

**"You got a letter if you managed to get into a game when the score was** undecided. It could be the last game. That happened with **Pat Ebbert**. He had a lot to do with winning our first McKinley game. He caused about three fumbles by hitting the center just as he was snapping the ball. So Pat won his letter just on the McKinley game."

**Chuck Mather**

**Massillon Championship Head Coach, 1948-53**
**Six Straight State Titles, Three National Titles**
**Head Coach, University of Kansas**
**Offensive Coordinator, Chicago Bears**

*—on developing a fair way to award football letters.*

**"Bob Kraus didn't particularly care for football. His dad was real forceful behind him. I always defended** it. A lot of mothers whipped kids to practice the piano. So what's wrong with a father giving the kid a hard time for football. Particularly in Massillon, because football is a college education for anybody who gets the grades. Bob became good enough that he got a scholarship to Purdue. When I went to Kansas he transferred there. His senior year he was one of my captains. He married one of the richest girls in Kansas.The point of the story is the old man, by being hard on him, really put him into a great life."

*Bob Kraus*

## Chuck Mather

**Massillon Championship Head Coach, 1948-53**
**Six Straight State Titles, Three National Titles**
**Head Coach, University of Kansas**
**Offensive Coordinator, Chicago Bears**

*—on a Massillon football success story.*

**"I was scared shitless. I was scared every game I ever played in—until somebody hit me."**

**Al Brown**

**Captain, All-Ohio Fullback, 1948**

*—on his feelings going into a football game.*

**"Bobby Dodd looked at our films in regard to a couple of our kids** he wanted at Georgia Tech. I was about to go to Kansas. He said, "Chuck, you *never* will get the technique in college that you have at Massillon. I didn't quite realize what he was talking about. But basically, you don't have kids going through junior high and high school, learning all these techniques. At Kansas, we got to where we didn't even try some of the stuff we were doing at Massillon."

**Chuck Mather**

**Massillon Championship Head Coach, 1948-53**
**Six Straight State Titles, Three National Titles**
**Head Coach, University of Kansas**
**Offensive Coordinator, Chicago Bears**

*—on legendary southern Coach Bobby Dodd's amazement over Massillon's downfield blocking technique.*

**"As a kid in grade school you see the players run out onto the field—** it leaves an everlasting impression on you. Pretty soon you're running out of your garage, pretending you're running onto Tiger field. I remember those days vividly, sitting up in the stands dreaming of being one of those guys. I'm sure kids still do it today."

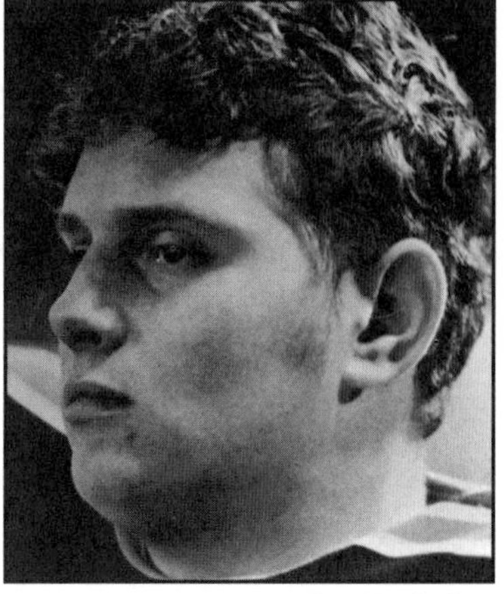

*Tim Ridgley*

**Tim Ridgley**

**All-Ohio, 1970**

*—on his first memory of Massillon football.*

**"Mike Takacs always looked like he was offside, because he always** got the jump on everybody."

**Jack Hill**

**Massillon Quarterback, 1946-48**

**Booster Club President, 1967**

*—on Massillon's Mike Takacs, an All-American guard at Ohio State.*

**"The coaches told us, 'If you come to football camp with blisters you're** going home.' If you didn't work out during the summer you'd end up with blisters. I never had blisters at camp—that was a dead giveaway."

**Lee Nussbaum**

**All-Ohio Running Back, 1952**

*—on the importance of coming to practice in shape.*

**"Bobby Hewitt sprained his ankle real bad. I carried him into his** house and layed him down on his bed. It was a flat-type frame with strands of wire hooked to a metal frame. He didn't have a mattress. He had a comforter folded over those wires. That was what he slept on. I later talked to Mrs. Hewitt and told her that we had a pretty decent mattress if she could use one. I told her I'd be glad to bring it over because we were getting a new one. He slept on that mattress from then on."

**Milan Chovan**

**Massillon halfback, 1945**

**Long-time Assistant Coach**

*—on an experience with Bobby Hewitt in junior high.*

## "I'm 15, I'm not even driving yet, I'm walking by his house every

Saturday night, trying to get up the nerve to go in there and ask him if he would teach me. Finally, I did. He took me in. He taught me. If it weren't for him, I wouldn't be where I am today."

*Steve Studer, Chris Spielman*

## Chris Spielman

**Massillon: 2-time All-Ohioan, All-American, 1983**
**USA Today Defensive Player of the Year, 1983**
**Ohio State: 2-time All-American, 1986-87**
**Lombardi Award Winner, 1987**
**NFL: Detroit Lions and Buffalo Bills, Since 1988**
**Four Pro Bowls**

*—on joining Steve Studer's weightlifting group.*

**TIGER TALES**

"Season ticket sales are always over 5,000. Game nights we sell a lot of tickets at the stadium. For big games we'll have 15,000-17,000 fans. We'll need nine people to sell tickets."

**JOSIE ROLLSTIN, TICKET MANAGER**

**"Dick Adams was a kid you had to run herd on a little bit. I always** started Bob Graber ahead of him and I think Dick figured he was better than Graber—and he probably was. But he wasn't as good of a punter and he wasn't as good a passer. But he was a better runner. A very elusive guy out there."

**Bud Houghton**

**Championship Head Coach, 1941, 1946-47**
**State Champs, 1941**
**Massillon Player, 1925-26**

*—on an early quarterback controversy in 1941.*

**"I got a job selling Coca Cola at the Rubber Bowl just to get in to see Massillon play. It was really** thrilling. That's when I said to myself, 'I want to play football. I want to play for Massillon. I want to come back home.' That's why I came back home."

**Irvin "Ace" Crable**

**Legendary Massillon Running Back, 1948-49**
**All-Ohio, Stark County Player of the Year, 1949**

*—on seeing Massillon play at the Akron Rubber Bowl as a child who had moved to Akron from Massillon.*

**"He was like trying to catch a dog in the middle of an open field. Art Hastings looked** like his hips went out of joint. I had great runners, but I don't know that I ever had any better than Art Hastings. Hastings was just outstanding."

Art Hastings

## Leo Strang

**Massillon Championship Head Coach, 1958-63**
**State Champs, 1959-61, Nat'l Champs 1959, '61**
**Head Coach, Kent State University**

*—on Massillon's all-time leading rusher, Art Hastings (3,090).*

**TIGER TALES**

**SIX MASSILLON PLAYERS NAMED ALL-OHIO FIRST TEAM TWO YEARS IN A ROW**

Bob Glass (1936-37), Don Snavely (1936-37), Horace Gillom (1939-40), Jim Russell (1939-40), Hase McKey (1958-59) and Chris Spielman (1982-83).

**"Going from high school straight to the pros, that was the wrong way,** but it was my way. I wouldn't want anyone else to try that."

**Willie Spencer**

**All-Ohio Running Back, 1971**
**World Football League Star, 1974-75, Memphis**
**NFL running back: Minnesota Vikings,**
**Washington Redskins, New York Giants**

*—on his unique route to professional football. He was only the third player to ever go straight from high school to professional football.*

**"I couldn't believe it, we had the players running the 100-yard dash** from one goal line to the other, and they were diving to be the first guy across the goal line. We'd get a whole bunch of guys running, and not just one guy was doing that. It was just unbelievable seeing this type of thing."

**Chuck Mather**

**Massillon Championship Head Coach, 1948-53**
**Six Straight State Titles, Three National Titles**
**Head Coach, University of Kansas**
**Offensive Coordinator, Chicago Bears**

*—on his first impression of Massillon players, 1948.*

**"I always felt that if I didn't give it 120 percent every time the ball** was snapped, I just wasn't going to make it. I wasn't very fast and I wasn't very big. I was a good student of the game—I knew I had to be. I'd do what the coaches said. I learned the fundamentals. I just tried as hard as I could every play. I owe a lot to football."

*David Canary*

## David Canary

**All-Ohio, 1956**
**All-American, University of Cincinnati, 1959**
**4-Time Emmy Winner, "All My Children"**
**"Candy" on "Bonanza"**

*—on his career as a Massillon Tiger.*

**"Bobby Herring weighed about 135 pounds. He was a wingback. He** came up to me in the 1959 Barberton game and said, 'Coach, I'm the only one who hasn't carried the ball.' There's about a minute to go in the game. I only had one running play for the wingback. I said, 'O.K. Bobby, get in and run your play.' I'll be damned if he didn't go 60 yards for a touchdown. That made it 90-0. We weren't trying to score. What can you do? You can't tell 'em not to play."

**Leo Strang**

**Massillon Championship Head Coach, 1958-63**
**State Champs, 1959-61, Nat'l Champs 1959, '61**
**Head Coach, Kent State University**

*—on Strang's 1959 squad that scored 431 points.*

**"You watch them perform at Tiger Stadium and you have the** attitude, 'Hey, I can be just like that. I can be as good as they are.' "

**David Whitfield**

**All-Ohio 1965**
**Captain, Ohio State, 1970**

*—on watching his brothers play at Tiger Stadium.*

**"Joe Sparma was a helluva nice kid. Handsome, good looking kid. Had a great arm. A lot of moxie."**

*Joe Sparma*

**Bo Schembechler**

**Legendary Michigan Head Coach**
**Ohio State Assistant Coach**

*—on Massillon's All-Ohio quarterback (1959) who quarterbacked Ohio State.*

**"Every time I tell someone I played at Massillon a feeling of pride comes over me."**

**Chris Spielman**

**Massillon: 2-time All-Ohioan, All-American,**
**USA Today Defensive Player of the Year, 1983**
**Ohio State: 2-time All-American,**
**Lombardi Award Winner**
**NFL: Detroit Lions, Buffalo Bills, Since 1988**
**Four Pro Bowls**

*—on Massillon pride.*

**"In my neighborhood we played a game that probably made me the** back I was. They called it 'Trip Travis.' I just ran back and forth down the field and the other kids tried to trip me. They'd come and get me and say, 'We're playing 'Trip Travis' today.' "

**Travis McGuire**

**All-Ohio Running Back, 1991**
**Stark County Player of the Year, 1991**
**Ohio Offensive Player of the Year, 1991**

*–on a childhood game that helped to develop running skills. McGuire is Massillon's single season rushing leader (1,976), single game rushing leader (302) and #3 all-time rusher (2,511).*

**"Bud Houghton evidently had heard that there was a fast, little** redhead out in Genoa. He came driving by when we were playing a touch football game one day. He talked me into coming in and enrolling in the Massillon school system."

**Tommy James**

**All-Ohio Halfback, 1940**
**Ohio State Captain-Elect, 1947**
**Member of the Cleveland Browns All-Time Team**

*—on being recruited to play for Massillon.*

*Jim Lawrence*

## "Someone came to me and said,

'Would you take Jim Lawrence back on the football team if there would never be a problem with him from this day forward?' I said, 'How can you guarantee that?' He said, 'I guarantee it.' I said, 'O.K., Jim Lawrence is back on the team.' Well, when we played Niles McKinley on Saturday night, he only knew two plays. He and the sweep. He scored on a 45-yard sweep that we pitched to him."

## Earle Bruce

**Massillon Championship Coach, 1964-65**
**State Champs, #2 in Nation, 1964-65**
**Head Coach, Ohio State University**

*—on his meeting with former Massillon and Ohio State star Charlie "Buut" Anderson. Lawrence scored Massillon's first touchdown in 1964's 14-8 win that ended Niles' 48-game unbeaten streak.*

**“Willie Spencer was a superstar in the World Football League.”**

**John McVay**
**All-Ohio Center, 1948**
**Head Coach, Memphis Southmen**
**Head Coach, New York Giants**
**Vice President and General Manager, San Francisco 49ers**

*—on former Massillon great Willie Spencer (1970-71).*

**“The other players refer to Willie Spencer as a bad dude. It is a** compliment of the highest order. He’s but 20 years old, the youngest player in all of professional football. He is the man **Larry Csonka** will have to beat out next season. It may not be easy. Willie is 6-4, 225-pounds and he runs...well, you need the Marines to bring him down. Scouts from the NFL can’t believe Willie is for real. Some have called him one of the best running backs in football.”

**George Lapidus**
**Memphis Press-Scimitar, 1974**

*—on Massillon’s Willie Spencer during his rookie season with the WFL’s Memphis Southmen.*

**"Dennis Franklin is one of the all-time great quarter-**backs at the University of Michigan. For three years he was 30-2-1, and never went to a bowl game. That's why a lot of people don't know how great Franklin was. In 1973 when we were undefeated and tied Ohio State, Denny was hit on a blitz and broke his collarbone. The Big Ten didn't think we could beat Southern Cal in the Rose Bowl without Denny, so they voted Ohio State to go. He was a great, great quarter-back."

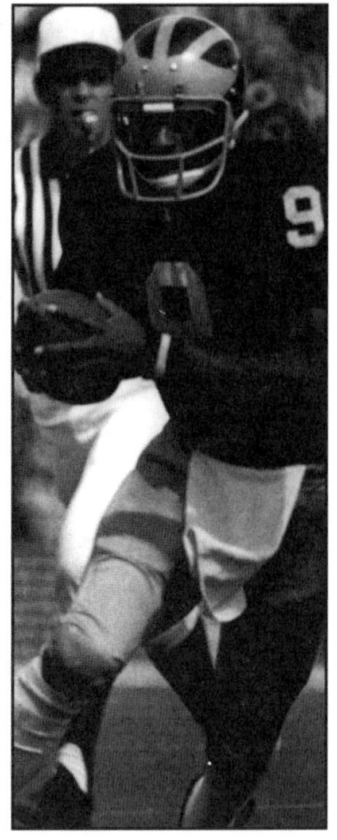

*Dennis Franklin at the University of Michigan.* (Photo courtesy of University of Michigan Archives).

## Bo Schembechler

**Legendary Michigan Head Coach**
**Ohio State Assistant Coach**

*—on Massillon's 1970 All-Ohio quarterback.*

**"Hase McKey was my idol. I wanted to be like him. That's where I set** my standards. I would watch that guy. He probably doesn't even know that. He made first team All-Ohio two years in a row. Only a couple of guys made All-Ohio two years in a row."

**"Big" Ben Bradley**

**All-American, All-Ohio Center, 1962**

*—on the player he looked up to.*

**"I singled out Ben Bradley, he was my hero. I'd go to the games with** my dad. I had this old pair of binoculars. I'd sit up there and focus in on Ben Bradley the whole game. As a little kid, I remember telling my dad, 'I want to play center for the Massillon Tigers.' That's because Ben Bradley was my idol."

**Steve Studer**

**Massillon Center, 1970-71**
**All-American Center, Bowling Green, 1975**
**Massillon Strength Coach**

*—on the player he looked up to.*

# Great Victories

## YOU REMEMBER THE BIG ONES

With 22 state championships and nine national titles, Massillon has a history of big wins. Many times the Massillon-Canton McKinley game has decided the state—and national—championship. But Massillon has a long history of classic matchups with other state and national powers.

Massillon's reputation as *Mighty Massillon,* and The Power of the state, made the team a target for up-and-coming teams throughout Ohio. Other towns would build winning programs, then challenge Massillon's supremacy.

Toledo Waite, Niles McKinley, Sharon, Pennsylvania and Cleveland Cathedral Latin all had significant unbeaten streaks snapped by Massillon.

The Tigers ended a 19-game roll when they beat Toledo Waite, 28-0, in 1940. Niles saw their 48- game unbeaten streak end in a 14-8 classic in the Akron Rubber Bowl in 1964. Massillon ended 17- game winning streaks against Sharon (37-20 in 1938), and Cleveland Cathedral Latin (40-13 in 1939).

**"I sat right next to the minister of the St. Paul's church, Reverend** Crites. McKinley got the ball down around the 20. He practically gave up then. I said, 'Don't give up yet, Reverend Crites, say a little prayer for the Tigers.' Just about that time, McKinley tried a pass and we intercepted—there were only minutes to go. A few plays later we passed for a touchdown and won the game."

**Luther Emery**

**Legendary Massillon Sportswriter**
**Editor of *The Independent***

*—on Massillon's thrilling 20-15 comeback win over McKinley in 1974.*

**"It was proven to Earle that night what we've always known.** How the Tiger spirit comes through. How they'll pull the unbelievable when it's least expected—the big plays."

**Milan Chovan**

**Massillon halfback, 1945**
**Longtime Assistant Coach**

*—on Massillon's 14-8 win over Niles in 1964 that ended Niles' 48-game unbeaten streak. It was Bruce's second game as Massillon coach.*

*Dave Sheegog falls over the goal line with the winning score in the 1964 Massillon-McKinley game.*

**"It was late in the third quarter. We were losing. Sometimes it takes** a little change—you see a spark when someone else comes in."

**David Sheegog**

**Star Massillon Quarterback, 1964-65**

*—on his role in the '64 McKinley game. Sheegog led Massillon to three second half touchdowns and a 20-14 win.*

**"Never in the history of this city has a victorious team been received so** enthusiastically. Three thousand people lined the streets, red fire was burned and Roman candles made the streets brilliant. The champions, headed by the city drum corps and the military band, marched through the streets of the city and were madly cheered by their townsmen. Business blocks and private residences were draped with the old gold and black colors of the Tigers, and the town was a bedlam until midnight."

***The Columbus Citizen,* 1903**

*—on the 1903 professional football championship.*

**"Altoona had Mike Reid. We had a double team on him. We ran an** off-tackle play and he threw **Denny Morgan** into our backfield. **Earle Bruce** said to me, 'What happened?' I said, 'Don't run any more plays that way. He threw our tackle right into our backfield.' The rest of the game we ran every play away from Mike Reid. He really cooled us down on that first play. We beat 'em 34-18."

**Carl "Ducky" Schroeder**

**Legendary Massillon Assistant, 1948-70**

**Massillon Player, 1923**

*—on future All-American and All-Pro Mike Reid.*

## "In 1972 we went down to play Upper Arlington in one of the classics. That's the highlight of my coaching career. Nothing's ever touched me as much as that Arlington win. Some people would say, 'What about McKinley?' McKinley's always different, you don't rate those with the rest. But that Arlington win was one of the highlights. Because they had beaten us a couple years before and took claim to the "new power" in the state of Ohio. We worked on that rascal for two or three years. And I think we played a team with better personnel than we had. They were certainly as well coached as we were. But the Massillon heritage—and it's there and it always will be there—that's the thing that came through and won it for us."

*Bob Commings*

**Bob Commings**

**Massillon Championship Coach, 1969-1973**
**State Champs, 1970**
**Head Coach, University of Iowa**

*—on his 1972 team's 14-0 win over Upper Arlington, who had won 77 of their last 80 games.*

**"1964 against Niles. I felt that was a real key game. We were in a lot** of arguments with Niles about who had the best football team. We really shut them up, you know, since we beat 'em 14-8. Yet we beat 'em with such tremendous odds against us. Because **Earle Bruce** was just a new coach here and he hadn't had hardly any time to put in his system. And it was the second game of the season. They had a new coach, but they hired one of their assistants. They had their same system. It just turned out that we were lucky enough—or good enough—to win that football game. But I always thought that was one of the great games that we played here."

**Carl "Ducky" Schroeder**

**Legendary Massillon Assistant, 1948-70**

**Massillon Player, 1923**

*—on the 1964 Massillon-Niles game at the Akron Rubber Bowl that ended Niles' 48-game unbeaten streak.*

*Scribes said it...*

The Boosters organize monstrous rallies and parades. Then, to make sure no one is deprived of his birthright, they telephone the scores at the end of each quarter to the factories whose workers can't get to the game.

**JEROME BRONDFIELD, SPORT MAGAZINE, 1951**

**"We took a special train to New Castle. It was rainin' when we** got on the train, it was rainin' when we got off. The stadium lights began poppin'. You could barely see by the end of the game. It just poured rain. My wife wore a blue suit, she had a white raincoat on. The raincoat was blue when we got back home."

**Luther Emery**

**Legendary Massillon Sportswriter**
**Editor of *The Independent***

*—on a legendary 1936 road win, 13-0, at New Castle, Pennsylvania.*

**"I got knocked out the first part of the 1952 game. I played most of** the game. After halftime I didn't know which end of the field was ours. I still played the third quarter. I didn't know the score. Never did know the score until I read the newspaper the next morning. I played a good game. Scored two touchdowns—should have had three, they stopped me on the one yard line."

**Lee Nussbaum**

**All-Ohio Running Back, 1952**

*—on playing the McKinley game with a concussion. Massillon won 41-8.*

**"In 1922 Massillon was 10-0 and won a great game against Cleveland** Shaw. In the last two minutes **Bill Edwards** kicked an extra point to win the game 7-6. Massillon had a great player on that team named **"Dutch" Hill**. He was the fullback. He later made a great name for himself at New York University as one of the great halfbacks in the history of that school."

**Carl "Ducky" Schroeder**

**Legendary Massillon Assistant, 1948-70**

**Massillon Player, 1923**

*—on Massillon's win over Shaw, that lead to Massillon's first state championship. Shaw was coached by former Massillon head coach John Snavely, who coached Massillon's first 10-0 team in 1916.*

**"We had rubber pants we put on. They got slick in the rain. We got** faster and they slowed down. They had regular pants on."

**Ray Getz**

**All-Ohio, 1939, Co-Captain, 1940**

*—on Massillon's uniform edge -vs- Toledo Waite in 1940. Massillon won the highly anticipated match-up 28-0 in a constant downpour.*

**"The first guy who came out of that runway** when they turned out the stadium lights and turned on the spotlight was **Tom Whitfield**. Altoona kept their team out on the field while we were introduced. And standing in the end of the runway was **Mike Reid**, this big tackle and fullback, who later was All-American at Penn State and All-Pro at Cincinnati. Reid said, 'You're going to get your ass beat tonight. We're going to run right over you.' Tom Whitfield said, while beating his chest, 'You might run one, you might run two, but the third time will be the last damn time you run.' I thought, 'Holy shit, that's a great answer.' "

*Tom Whitfield*

**Earle Bruce**

**Massillon Championship Coach, 1964-65**
**State Champs, #2 in Nation, 1964-65**
**Head Coach, Ohio State University**

*—on Massillon's first meeting with Altoona, PA. A win.*

**"I was the last man to carry the ball against Warren. The clock** showed 57 seconds. I was looking up at the clock and **Joe Sparma's** coming onto the field saying, 'Get up Ives, get up, we've got time.' The clock showed 1:58. You tell me if that clock ain't wrong."

**Ivory Benjamin**
**Legendary Massillon Running Back, 1955-57**
**All American, All-Ohio and Stark County**
**Player of the Year, 1957**

*—on the "clock game" against Warren in 1957. Massillon won 20-14.*

**"I can say to the Massillon people that they have one of the greatest** teams I've ever seen. I think if we could pick up a team of the finest players of Tiger opponents this season, we might hold the Massillon team to a 7-0 victory. I doubt, though, if we could beat them."

**Jack Mollenkopf**
**Toledo Waite Head Coach**
**Legendary Purdue Coach**

*—on his feelings after Massillon's 28-0 win over his Toledo Waite team. The win ended Waite's 19 game winning streak.*

*All-Ohio end Clyde Childers, who caught the pass that won the "clock game" against Warren in 1957.*

**"Joe Sparma threw the ball** and **Clyde Childers** didn't quite catch it. He kind of volleyballed it across the goal line and finally caught it in the end zone. That put us ahead 20-14 and the game was over. I was spotting the game from the top of the stadium. Of course when it gets that close you're watching the clock all the time. I never saw anything happen to the clock."

## Carl "Ducky" Schroeder

**Legendary Massillon Assistant, 1948-70**
**Massillon Player, 1923**

*—on the "clock game" of 1957. Warren supporters say the clock gave Massillon an extra minute to win.*

**"Lenny Dawson was quite a quarterback. We beat them over** there one time, it had to heartbreaking, but he came over to our team bus and said 'You fellas played a great game.'"

**Chuck Mather**

**Massillon Championship Head Coach, 1948-53**
**Six Straight State Titles, Three National Titles**
**Head Coach, University of Kansas**
**Offensive Coordinator, Chicago Bears**

*—on the former Alliance, Purdue, Kansas City Chiefs and Hall of Fame quarterback who never beat Massillon.*

**"The Massillon crowd gave the Bacon team a standing ovation** when they left the field because it was such a good football game. We were used to beating people by big scores. We weren't used to eight to nuthin.' "

**Leo Strang**

**Massillon Championship Head Coach, 1958-63**
**State Champs, 1959-61, Nat'l Champs, 1959, '61**
**Head Coach, Kent State University**

*—on Massillon's 8-0 win over Cincinnati Roger Bacon at Tiger Stadium in 1960. Massillon gave Bacon its only losses in 1960 and 1961.*

*Nick Pribich is ready to kick the winning extra point.*

**"I'd always practice with my dad, and the last kick would always be to beat McKinley in the 100th game.**

All I remember is running out there. My whole body was pretty numb, I was really nervous. When I got out there, **Willie Spencer** came up to me and grabbed my face mask and said, 'Come on Pribich, come on Pribich, you've gotta make this kick.' I knew it would be a perfect snap and hold. As soon as I kicked it, it was like the greatest feeling ever. I turned around and ran and just got mobbed by my teammates."

**Nick Pribich**

**Massillon Kicker, 1994**

*—on his kick to give Massillon a 42-41 overtime win over Canton McKinley in the 100th game.*

**"I never saw a locker room like that one. Before the game, you could** hear a pin drop. **Dick Scholem**, who did our play-by-play on the radio, looked at the team and he said, 'Coach, what's wrong?' I said, 'I don't know what's going to happen. But if I were to guess, I think a real good football team is going to get the shit kicked out of them.' We were ahead 30-0 at the half. We held **Paul Warfield** to minus yardage. It was unbelievable."

**Leo Strang**

**Massillon Championship Head Coach, 1958-63**
**State Champs, 1959-61, Nat'l Champs, 1959, '61**
**Head Coach, Kent State University**

*—on Massillon's 38-8 win over Warren in 1959.*

**"We played Warren and we held Paul Warfield to a minus seven gained.** That was one of the greatest games we ever played. Warren came to Tiger Stadium undefeated, we were undefeated. At halftime we had 'em beat 30-0. I don't recall any time we were any more fired up for a game."

**Carl "Ducky" Schroeder**

**Legendary Massillon Assistant, 1948-70**
**Massillon Player, 1923**

*—on Massillon's 38-8 win over Warren and their star back Paul Warfield, who became an NFL Hall of Famer.*

# Heartbreakers

## LOSSES YOU CAN'T FORGET

When your team has a history of winning most of its games (.834 since 1932), it's the losses that linger. Especially the close losses—the heart-breakers. Massillon has suffered 13 one-point losses in its 100-plus seasons.

*Obie offers consolation*

And it's a safe bet that the fans, players and coaches who remember those games still feel the pain—no matter how many years it's been.

It's an understatement to say that *all* losses are painful to Massillon fans. Massillon losses are often described with words like death, disbelief, sadness—you get the picture. And it doesn't take a newcomer long to find out that the most painful and unforgivable losses are those to Canton McKinley. Wobegone is the coach who loses to Canton McKinley; there is no excuse good enough. Only victory is acceptable in Massillon.

**"Chuck [Mather] lost one game in 1948 and one in 1949 and** both teams were coached by former Massillon football players. **Mel Knowlton** coached Alliance. He quarterbacked Brown's first team. **Augie Morningstar** coached Mansfield, he was Brown's captain in 1935. Chuck lost once to Warren. He was 57-3 and won the state championship all the years he was here."

**Luther Emery**

**Legendary Massillon Sportswriter**
**Editor of *The Independent***

*—on Chuck Mather's three losses at Massillon.*

**"We kept poundin' and poundin' and they kept poundin' and poundin'. We** figured, 'Hey, pretty soon they're gonna give.' But they never did give. That was a sad weekend in Massillon. Oh, that was a sad weekend in Massillon. And it had to be **Augie Morningstar**, of all people."

**Irvin "Ace" Crable**

**Legendary Massillon Running Back, 1948-49**
**All-Ohio, Stark County Player of the Year, 1949**

*—on 1949's 16-12 loss to Mansfield. Former Massillon coach Augie Morningstar (1945) was Mansfield's coach.*

**"That Upper Arlington game, we should have won. We had them 6-0, and we're on the one-yard-line. It's third down and we had an off-tackle play called and the quarterback checked off. You don't check off down there. He checked off to the quarterback sneak and we jumped. We got a five-yard penalty and we didn't score. They ran a reverse on fourth and nine and took it in for a touchdown. They kicked the extra point and beat us 7-6 and won the state title."**

*Nick Vrotsos*

## Nick Vrotsos

**Legendary Massillon Assistant, 1958-84**

*—on a changed play in Massillon's only loss in 1967.*

**"I remember Dave Canary crying in the locker room. He was just** sittin' down wiping his eyes with a towel. A good many Massillon boys there were crying. They had built up their hopes and nerves. This was quite a letdown for them. It didn't show any weakness on their part to cry. A nervous letdown. Coach Harp was going around trying to console them. We were trying to console coach Harp. He was going along patting them on the back."

**Luther Emery**

**Legendary Massillon Sportswriter**
**Editor of *The Independent***

*—on the scene in the Massillon locker room following their heartbreaking 13-7 loss to Canton McKinley in 1955.*

**"Losing the St. Ignatius game was devastating. I was pretty well crushed."**

**Travis McGuire**

**All-Ohio Running Back, 1991**
**Stark County Player of the Year, 1991**
**Ohio Offensive Player of the Year, 1991**

*—on Massillon's 14-13 semi-finals loss to Cleveland St. Ignatius in 1991.*

**“That game decimated a lot of people. I remember crying. Those** were bitter tears after the McKinley game. We just felt partly that we’d been cheated by the fates. It was as if God had conspired to humble us or something. We just felt that powers that were stronger than us had come down and played a hand in that. By the second half you couldn’t move. It was a bunch of guys wallowing around in this wet, snowy, whitish, blackish, muddy thing. We lost the state championship because of two passes from center from two different centers, one they fell on in the end zone, the other on about the one yard line. They beat us 13-7. Nobody blamed the centers. It was like trying to pick up a mud ball and throw it back 20 yards. It was a quagmire.”

**David Canary**

**All-Ohio, 1956**
**All-American, University of Cincinnati, 1959**
**4-Time Emmy Winner, “All My Children”**
**“Candy” on “Bonanza”**

*—on the 13-7 loss to Canton McKinley in 1955.*

**“We took the bus to the Elks Club in Warren to get something to eat.** The Warren fans had formed a ring around our bus and circled around and around. They wouldn’t let us off. We had to get the police in there to help us off the bus so we could have dinner.”

**Tom Straughn**

**Massillon Player, 1950-51**
**Booster Club President, 1963**

*—on the scene in Warren, following Massillon’s heartbreaking 19-13 loss to Warren in 1951.*

**“We were the best team in the state at that time. We were playing one** of the best teams in the country in Cleveland St. Ignatius. I think we were better. We turned the ball over twice inside the 20. We scored late and tried to pooch kick it and it didn’t work. I got a lot of criticism over that call. But I would make the same call again. It was a great game. They just put a great drive together at the end to win.”

**Lee Owens**

**Massillon Head Coach, 1988-91**
**Head Coach Akron University**

*—on Massillon’s 14-13 loss to Cleveland St. Ignatius in the State Semifinal game, 1991.*

# Community

## IN MASSILLON, EVERYONE'S A TIGER

It's hard to estimate how many games were won during the opponent's bus ride through downtown Massillon. Driving down Lincoln Way, the town's main thoroughfare, opposing players see the orange and black flags that line the street. A series of road signs that point the way to Tiger Stadium give visitors the feeling that football is "big time" in this town.

Virtually every store window proudly displays an oversized Massillon football schedule and a sign urging the Tigers to victory. An award-winning football mural adorns the side of a downtown building. A huge downtown sign elegantly displays the season schedule.

Two miles from the stadium you begin to encounter traffic. Are all these people going to the football game?

Approaching the stadium, it's a circus atmosphere. Policemen directing traffic. A sea of orange-clad fans blanket the landscape. There is electricity in the air. The Massillon community is doing its job.

**"I played for them. I played for Massillon, for the town, consciously,** not subconsciously. Hey, I didn't want this guy going home, or going to work at Superior's, thinking, 'Man, we shouldn't have lost.' I wanted to carry that burden for them and make them go to work happy. Make them proud to wear their Tiger stuff around."

**Chris Spielman**

**Massillon: 2-time All-Ohioan, All-American,**
**USA Today Defensive Player of the Year, 1983**
**Ohio State: 2-time All-American,**
**Lombardi Award Winner, 1983**
**NFL: Detroit Lions, Buffalo Bills, Since1988**
**Four Pro Bowls**

*—on his desire to play for the people of Massillon.*

**"The people were probably a little bit anxious, primarily because we didn't beat Canton."**

**Paul E. Brown**

**Massillon Quarterback, 1923-25**
**Championship Coach: Massillon Tigers,**
**Ohio State Buckeyes and Cleveland Browns**
**Coach of 14 Championship Teams**
**Founder of the Cincinnati Bengals**

*—on public pressure after he had lost to Canton twice.*

**"In some respects I was a community project. My mother was ill** a lot. I lived on the Hill, I lived on Tremont Street, I lived with the Tolles family in a foster home and I lived with Mrs. Dandridge. I had a lot of people touch my life in a variety of ways. I think all for the good."

**Homer Floyd**

**Legendary Massillon Running Back, 1952-54,**
**All-Ohio, 1954**
**University of Kansas star, 1955-58**

*—on his upbringing in Massillon.*

**"There are so many people in this town that football has saved. And** it has no racial preference. You know as many white young people and black young people who are walking these streets, making their way, because football has touched them. They are good, solid human beings. And when things get tough they can rely on the values they learned at Tiger Stadium. That may sound gung-ho to some people, but I believe that with all my heart."

**Bob Commings**

**Massillon Championship Head Coach, 1969-73**
**State Champs, #2 in Nation, 1970**

*—on football's profound positive effect in Massillon.*

**"Football is very important to the city. It's a rallying point. In terms** of enthusiasm and togetherness, through the bad times economically and the good times. It's always been a rallying point for the community. It's what separates this city from other cities across the country. Football games are a community activity and a family activity. So many people have their children with them, or their aunt with them or their mother with them. You have a strong cross-section of the community."

**Mayor Francis Cicchinelli**

**Massillon Alumnus**

*—on football's importance to the city of Massillon.*

**Football is bred in Massillonians. The native citizen has heard it talked** from the time he opened his eyes in the cradle, and new residents have frequently been bored to tears with the boasts of the old guard until they, too, became convinced that there's something more than usual about the game as it is played here, when a whole community enters into the spirit of the thing."

**Luther Emery**

**Legendary Massillon Sportswriter**

**Editor of *The Independent***

*—on the Massillon community.*

**"In junior high you're never in the newspaper, you're never talked** about on the radio. But as a sophomore people were coming up to me saying, 'Hey, I heard about you on the radio or I read about you in the *Akron Beacon Journal* or the *Cleveland Plain Dealer.* Or people in restaurants, you're out with your buddies at Burger Chef, people would look at ya and whisper. It was like, do I have food on my mouth or something?"

**Chris Spielman**

**Massillon: 2-time All-Ohioan, All-American,**
**USA Today Defensive Player of the Year, 1983**
**Ohio State: 2-time All-American,**
**Lombardi Award Winner**
**NFL: Detroit Lions, Buffalo Bills, Since 1988**
**Four Pro Bowls**

*—on Massillon's reaction to their young star.*

**"I was in all kinds of trouble when I was a kid. I was what you'd call** a menace to the community. Football is what got me straightened out."

**Irvin "Ace" Crable**

**Legendary Massillon Running Back, 1948-49**
**All-Ohio, Stark County Player of the Year, 1949**

*—on Massillon football's positive influence.*

**"It's a horrible thing to admit, but when your kid's playing ball you're** worried more about them making a mistake than you are about them getting hurt. That's a horrible thing for a parent to have to admit, but in this town—with the pressure and all—it's true.

**Jim Snively**
**Team Dentist**
**School Board President**

*—on the pressure of having your son play for Massillon.*

**"Here was a steel mill town. I thought it was a beautiful town.** The people who were from Massillon all thought that, too. The people there knew each other. It was big enough that things were going on. The high school was a big part of what was going on. People related to that because their kids were involved."

**Mike Brown**
**Coach Paul Brown's Son**
**General Manager, Cincinnati Bengals**

*—on his impression of Massillon.*

**"You had to do better. You didn't want to go to the steel mills. After** football season was over—I hate to say it—especially the black guys, they were through. That was pumped into my head. *You have to go on.* My parents pushed me to go on to school. I was determined. I saw a lot of them fail. I didn't want that to happen to me. Massillon had a lot of black athletes, once they finished football, they were finished. I definitely didn't want that. I had good influences from my parents and the church."

**"Big" Ben Bradley**

**All-American, All-Ohio Center, 1962**

*—on positive influences in his home and community.*

**"I talked to at least 100 people in all walks of life, and everyone talked** about and praised one thing, the Tigers of Massillon High School, and I said to myself, 'Grant Murray, you are in the perfect high school city, perhaps the only one of its kind in the world.' "

**Grant Murray**

**Vice President, Toledo School Board**

*—on a fall visit to Massillon in 1940.*

**"There's no better place to coach in the world. *No better place.* The** best pay. The best treatment. Best side benefits. I can't reveal some of them. One of them was the automobile every year. All of the theatres for nothing, the bowling alleys for nothing. Pass to the swimming club, the Elms Country Club, invited to all kinds of things. The Booster Club always took good care of me. I know I took a cut to come to Kent State."

**Leo Strang**

**Massillon Championship Head Coach, 1958-63**
**State Champs, 1959-61, Nat'l Champs 1959, '61**
**Head Coach, Kent State University**

*—on the Massillon coaching job.*

**"What most amazed me about Massillon is that they really love** their kids. They care about 'em. That's what I like about Massillon. There's no bullshit about that."

**Earle Bruce**

**Championship Coach, 1964-65**
**State Champs, #2 in Nation, 1964-65**
**Head Coach, Ohio State University, 1979-86**

*—on what makes Massillon, Massillon.*

**"There are two industries that donate their time to put up the** Massillon Tiger flags downtown. One company puts them up and the other one takes them down."

**Gene Boerner**

**President, Massillon Chamber of Commerce**
**Booster Club President, 1973**

*—on the support of local industry for the Tigers.*

**"I'm the most fortunate black guy who ever left that high school. After** high school I became a drunk. I went to the penitentiary and came home—and I was a drunk. And I was a damn good drunk. But the people of this town would still give me just about anything I asked for. The people liked me. I was getting clothes when I needed them. I was still getting money when I needed it. They didn't forget me. Now I haven't had a drink in 14 years. And I haven't had a cigarette in nine years. I've got that respect back."

**Ivory Benjamin**

**Legendary Massillon running back, 1955-57**
**All American, All-Ohio and Stark County**
**Player of the Year, 1957**

*—on the loyalty of the Massillon community.*

**"It was such a wonderful experience being here in Massillon. It was the** first town I ever got involved with any kind of community life. The Lions Club, the drum and bugle corps, the barbershop quartet. It was through those sort of things that I got more involved in the community life until, truly, Massillon seemed home to me. I wish I'd never left it."

**George "Red" Bird**

**Band Director, 1938-45**
**Entertainment Director, Cleveland Browns**
**Entertainment Director, Cincinnati Bengals**

*—on becoming part of the Massillon community.*

**The first day I was there L.J. Smith took me around to meet the people** of Massillon. Within the first week they had a welcome party. I must have met 10,000 people. It was unlike any other place I'd ever coached."

**Leo Strang**

**Massillon Championship Head Coach, 1958-63**
**State Champs, 1959-61, Nat'l Champs 1959, '61**
**Head Coach, Kent State University**

*—on his baptism to Massillon football.*

**"Back in those days all the doctors in town offered their services to take** care of any injuries we had with our kids. Even down to the junior high. If a kid got hurt in practice we'd take 'em down to the doctor's office. Any time you took 'em in their services were free. This was true of all the doctors in town. This was back in the Depression era."

**Bud Houghton**

**Championship Head Coach, 1941, 1946-47**
**State Champs, 1941**
**Massillon Player, 1925-26**

*—on the cooperation of local physicians.*

**"Maurie and Katie Basler were great boosters. They'd take in 3-4** games a week. They'd go to the junior high game on Thursday, the high school game on Friday night and be down at Ohio State on Saturday afternoon and be up to the Browns games on Sunday."

**Luther Emery**

**Legendary Massillon Sportswriter**
**Editor of *The Independent***

*—on Massillon's super-boosters.*

**"Rider's Drug Store was a hang-out for some of the top boosters.** One night when they were in the course of enlarging the stadium in 1934, I was up there. **Dr. H.W. Bell** was always a strong booster. He and I and a couple of others were wondering if they were leaving enough elevation between rows so the person behind could see over the person ahead. So there was nothing to do but to go down and find out. It was about 11 p.m. and we went down to the field. They were still hammering away. And old Doc Bell would sit in a seat. 'Now Lute, you're short, so you sit behind me. Can you see the field?' I'd say, 'Yeah, I can see the field, Doc.' We'd move over to another section, and that went on 'til we'd almost worked our way around the stadium."

**Luther Emery**

**Legendary Massillon Sportswriter**
**Editor of *The Independent***

*—on a late-night rendezvous with "Doc" Bell in 1934.*

*Scribes said it...*

It's easy to see why Massillon might well be termed the "high school football capital of the world." Washington High and its gridiron Tigers are the big news here. They come first and the town's business and social life hinges around them.

**JACK SENN, *TOLEDO TIMES,* 1940**

**"In my business I meet a lot of people who have wealth, some of** them are genuinely sophisticated, worldly people. But people talk to me and say, 'You're a nice guy.' The nice guy, that comes from Massillon. If I was from somewhere else I would be a different person. I think the values that were instilled in me there and the common touch are something Massillon taught me. The people in Massillon are as good as anybody anywhere in the world. That's why I like Massillon."

**David Canary**

**All-Ohio, 1956**
**All-American, University of Cincinnati, 1959**
**4-Time Emmy Winner, "All My Children"**
**"Candy" on "Bonanza"**

*—on the Massillon community.*

**The majority of the town is blue collar. These people are willing to make sacrifices to see that their kids have all the best."**

**Rick Shepas**

**New Massillon Tigers Head Coach**

*—on Massillon's commitment to their youth.*

**"The Massillon football team infects and invades the whole town. It affects** so many kids at a very early age. It gets people out and gets them together. It's something everybody can get behind and root for. It's in the papers. It's all-pervasive, it's everywhere—it's good."

**David Canary**

**All-Ohio, 1956**
**All-American, University of Cincinnati, 1959**
**4-Time Emmy Winner, "All My Children"**
**"Candy" on "Bonanza"**

*—on Massillon's emphasis on football.*

**"You'd go to the barber shop or the grocery store and people would** say, 'We're going to be good this year, aren't we.' I'd say, 'Oh, yeah, sure.' "

**John McVay**

**All-Ohio Center, 1948**
**Head Coach, Memphis Southmen**
**Head Coach, New York Giants**
**Vice President and General Manager, San Francisco 49ers**

*—on the townspeople's interest in the team.*

# Massillon Fans

## LOYAL, KNOWLEDGEABLE, FANATICAL

Massillon football fans are as famous as the football team and band they support. It's a well known fact that many visiting teams experience "stage fright" when they run onto the field at Paul Brown Tiger Stadium, with a capacity near 20,000. And those big crowds not only intimidate visiting schools, they inspire the home team to victory.

Massillon's attendance records are almost unbelievable. The Massillon Tigers have played before 8 million fans. Tiger games have averaged over 18,000 fans per game over a 10-game schedule. In 1945 the Massillon-Cleveland Cathedral Latin game drew 51,000 fans to Cleveland Stadium.

Since the 1930s, fans by the thousands have routinely braved cold, rainy weather to happily wait in line for hours for a chance to buy tickets to big games. Only the size of the stadium has kept Massillon from posting even higher attendance.

Some people say Massillon fans expect a lot, that they're fanatical, that they don't like to lose. It's true. But they also say they're the best fans in the world.

**"Massillon fans know football. They follow the kids, starting at** elementary, all the way up. Half of 'em probably *played* football. I don't care how old they are, they know when a coach calls the wrong play or is playing the wrong player. You just don't get away with anything with the Massillon fans. They can see it."

**David Sheegog**

**Star Massillon Quarterback, 1964-65**

*—on Massillon fans.*

*Scribes said it...*

**Fans Stand in Heavy Downpour and Fight to See Tigers Romp Over Boastful Toledo Waite**

Twenty-two thousand persons packed Massillon's stadium in a driving rain to see the mighty Massillon Tigers prove Toledo Waite doesn't belong in the same league with them. From 2,000 to 3,000 others were turned away, some so mad that they wanted to fight the gatekeepers and tear down the stadium walls. It was the first time in memory that heavy rain has spurred additional thousands into attempting admission to a football game sold out for a week. Waite's state championship claims were washed into the storm sewers as the Tigers rolled to a 28-0 win, their 31st in a row.

**JIM SCHLEMMER, *AKRON BEACON JOURNAL*, 1940**

*Massillon fans exult after a touchdown in the 100th Massillon-McKinley game, a 42-41 Massillon win.*

**"Massillon fans are loyal. Of course you always have a few knockers and bleacher coaches, but I think the fans have been very loyal to the program."**

**Luther Emery**

**Legendary Massillon Sportswriter**
**Editor of *The Independent***

*—on the loyalty of Massillon fans.*

**"Great fans. Kind of tilted toward victory. Supportive, yet critical."**

**Earle Bruce**

**Championship Coach, 1964-65**
**State Champs, #2 in Nation, 1964-65**
**Head Coach, Ohio State University**

*—on Massillon fans.*

**"Massillon fans probably have a better knowledge of high school football than any community in the country."**

**Gerry Faust**

**Cincinnati Moeller, Head Coach**
**Notre Dame, Head Coach**

*—on Massillon fans.*

**"The fans were great to me. I'd hate to be there and lose."**

**Leo Strang**

**Massillon Championship Head Coach, 1958-63**
**State Champs, 1959-61, Nat'l Champs 1959, '61**
**Head Coach, Kent State University**

*—on Massillon fans.*

# "All the boys hadda pee, and they didn't think of Massillon scoring.

*Horace Gillom*

They were back in the lavatory when they heard this shout go up from the Massillon side. **Horace Gillom** batted the ball with one hand, got it with the other hand and scored a touchdown to tie the game right at the end of the half. And the boys came running out of the lavatory with their pants down. Half of the stands came running out of the lavatory.

## Luther Emery

**Legendary Massillon Sportswriter**
**Editor of *The Independent***

*—on a Tommy James to Horace Gillom TD pass that "literally" caught Massillon fans with their pants down during the cold 1940 Massillon-McKinley game.*

**"Doc Bell was one of our most ardent football fans. On his death bed he had me calling from the press box during a football game to tell him the score by quarters. The last time I called, Mrs. Bell said, 'He's in a coma.' "**

**Luther Emery**

**Legendary Massillon Sportswriter**
**Editor, *The Independent***

*—on Massillon Board of Education President and physician, Doc Bell.*

**"The superintendent of schools used to lead cheers in the 1920s.** When things got bad for the home team the students would yell for **H.R. Gorrell** and he'd lead cheers. They always felt that did something for the team."

**Bud Houghton**

**Championship Head Coach, 1941, 1946-47**
**State Champs, 1941**

*—on Massillon football games in the 1920's.*

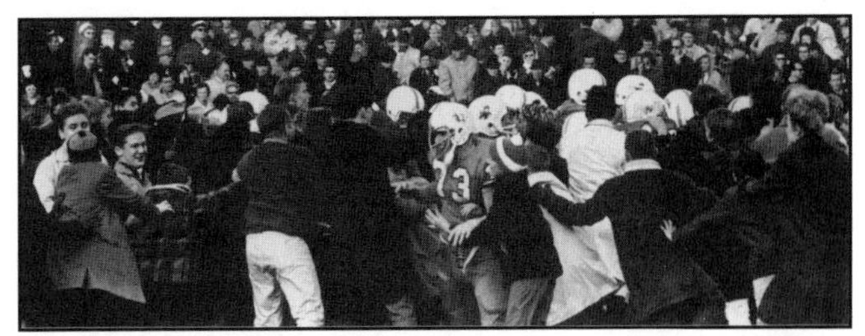

*Massillon students form a tunnel for players in 1965.*
(Photo by Canton Repository)

**"When I ran out of the locker room to start the second half, all of our** student body had come down on the field and made a tunnel. Now you have never seen that kind of support. You know people support you when you're 14-0 ahead. When you're 14-0 down, some people get down. Our students were all lined up. We ran through them. I said, 'My God, if they haven't given up, why should I give up?' We went back and worked and we won that game."

**Earle Bruce**

**Championship Coach, 1964-65**
**State Champs, #2 in Nation, 1964-65**
**Head Coach, Ohio State University, 1979-87**

*—on Massillon fans at the McKinley game, 1965. Massillon came back to win, 18-14.*

**"We came walking in the stadium. The Massillon people were there** early—it was a sea of orange and black on the other side of the stadium. We had to walk by them to get to the locker room. They all stood up and yelled, 'We want Moeller, we want Moeller.' I stood right there as our kids walked by and said, 'Keep your ears open and your mouths shut.' "

**Gerry Faust**

**Cincinnati Moeller, Head Coach**
**Notre Dame, Head Coach**

*—on Massillon fans before the state playoff finals against Cincinnati Moeller in 1980. Massillon lost,30-7.*

*Scribes said it...*

Another chapter in Massillon High football was written into the books today in indelible print. Certainly one of the greatest football towns in the country, Massillon again demonstrated its amazing loyalty to its high school team last night when 22,000 persons sat and stood in a cold, drenching rain to watch the Tigers conquer Toledo Waite, 28-0 in the super-special schoolboy grid game of the year.

**HENRY ANDREWS, *THE CLEVELAND PRESS,* 1940**

# Great Teams

## THE 1940 TEAM STANDS OUT, BUT 21 OTHERS WERE STATE CHAMPIONS

Massillon has endured just one losing season in 67 years (through 1997). Twenty-three Tiger teams have gone through the regular season undefeated. Twenty-one teams have finished with one loss. Eighteen lost two games. And the Tigers have always taken pride in their tough schedule.

Because of their winning tradition, Massillon faces opponents week-in, week-out that are "up" for the game. In most cases, Massillon is the biggest game on their opponent's schedule.

It is a subjective subject. But it's fair to say that all 22 state championship teams are among the great ones. Other great teams were tripped up along the way—some by better teams, others by a twist of fate.

Considering that 62 Massillon teams have lost two games or less—great teams by most standards—it seems fair to say that there have been too many great teams to mention in Massillon history.

**"I often wondered whether my Ohio State team that first year, which** lost one game, 14-7, to Northwestern, could have beaten our '40 team here in Massillon. Our '40 team was much faster. Ohio State would be bigger. I coached both teams. I used to wonder about it, thinking of some of our players. **Pokey Blunt, Lindell Houston, Horace Gillom,** a lot of these guys became fine pro players. Blunt was the most deceiving fella, tremendous jet speed. If I compared him to the guy who was playing for me at Ohio State it would have been no contest as far as being a long shot running back was concerned. It's a thing that's crossed my mind more than once."

**Paul E. Brown**

**Massillon Quarterback, 1923-25**
**Championship Coach: Massillon Tigers, Ohio State Buckeyesand Cleveland Browns**
**Coach of 14 Championship Teams**
**Founder, Coach, GM, Cincinnati Bengals**

*—on thoughts of a match-up between his 1941 Buckeyes and 1940 Tigers.*

*The 1909 Tigers, Massillon's first undefeated team.*

**"The football team had been firmly established in their claim of champions of the state and nothing** was too good for them. Honors were showered upon them from every direction and no less than four banquets tendered them by enthusiastic citizens of the town."

**Massillon Yearbook, 1910**

*—on the undefeated 1909 Tigers (9-0-1), who are not recognized as state champions by Massillon historians.*

**"Clarence Johnson was a big horse. Al Brown was a tough-ass fullback.** **'Ace' Crable** was a will-o'-the-wisp, **Dick Jacobs** was sort of a slashing runner. **Jack Hill** had a variety of skills, he could run, he could throw a ball through a wall, he could kick."

**John McVay**

**All-Ohio Center, 1948**
**Head Coach, Memphis Southmen**
**Head Coach, New York Giants**
**Vice President and General Manager, San Francisco 49ers**

*—on the backfield of the 1948 state champions. McVay was starting center.*

**TIGER TALES**

"It all starts in first grade, the week of the Canton McKinley game. The first graders all write letters to the players. They draw a picture at the top of the paper and right a little story below it. Then they bring Obie, the live tiger, around to the schools. Some years the players and cheerleaders come around. The students dress in orange and black that whole week. The teachers do, too. Some of the schools take part in the Beat McKinley parade."

**RUSS RAMSEY, FORMER ASSISTANT COACH AND ELEMENTARY SCHOOL PRINCIPAL**

*The 1916 Tigers, the first undefeated/untied team.*

**"Massillon has every right in claiming the championship of Ohio.**

In three years, Coach **John Snavely's** Massillon teams are 24-3. They have scored 623 points to 72 for their opponents. Often, in scrimmages, he puts on a suit and takes spills as well as gives them, but, through all this, his word is law and is obeyed to the letter."

***The Massillonian,* 1916**

*—on Massillon's first 10-0 team, which is not recognized as state champion by Massillon historians.*

**"I don't think we had a man on that 1948 team who weighed 200** pounds. We were really small. But we were tough, I'll tell ya. We were what you call street fighters. I lived in "the bottoms." The houses were so close together you could step off of one porch onto the other. We always had a conflict with what we called "the hill." But when we got down to Washington High School we all became as one. The fightin' and feudin' was over. Coach Mather made a team out of us. He put that team together beautifully. He made us more streamlined—like a Cadillac. We went from the single wing to the T-formation. It was beautiful."

**Irvin "Ace" Crable**

**Legendary Massillon Running Back**
**All-Ohio, Stark County Player of the Year, 1949**

*—on the 1948 state champions—coach Chuck Mather's first team.*

*Scribes Said it...*

When we add them up we find that 15 of the 22 senior members of the 1950 football team are going to college this fall—with the help of football.

**LUTHER EMERY**
***THE EVENING INDEPENDENT*, 1950**

**"That 1922 team was so great. They were undefeated. They had** a fella named Edwin Hill. They called him **'Dutch' Hill.** He was the big star of that team. He was big and burly. Walked with a swagger. Played fullback. We thought he was great because he normally plowed over everybody."

*Edwin "Dutch" Hill*

## Bud Houghton

**Championship Head Coach, 1941, 1946-47**
**State Champs, 1941**
**Massillon Player, 1925-26**

*—on Massillon's first state championship team in 1922. Hill is still Massillon's single season scoring leader (204).*

**"Purdue coach Jack Mollenkopf said the greatest downfield blocking team in the United States—pro, college or high school—is Massillon High School."**

**Carl "Ducky" Schroeder**
**Legendary Massillon Assistant, 1948-70**
**Massillon Player, 1923**

*—on the great downfield blocking teams fielded by Chuck Mather between 1948-53.*

**"We thought we were truly great, great football coaches. Come to** find out four years later that six of our players had opportunities to play professional football . So we weren't as hot as we thought we were."

**Bob Commings**
**Massillon Championship Head Coach, 1969-73**
**State Champs, #2 in Nation, 1970**
**Head Coach, University of Iowa, 1974**

*—on the talented 1970 State Champion Tigers.*

**"Right before the McKinley game, Jim Muzzi asked Joe Sparma who** was the best team he played against all year. Sparma's remark was 'Our second team.' Muzzi about dropped his teeth."

**Leo Strang**

**Massillon Championship Head Coach, 1958-63**
**State Champs, 1959-61, Nat'l Champs 1959, '61**
**Head Coach, Kent State University**

*—on Massillon's great 1959 state and national championship team. Sparma was the All-Ohio quarterback. Muzzi was the famed WHBC radio broadcaster.*

**"We went to scrimmage Kent State. We all got on the bus with our prac-**tice uniforms and shoulder pads. We get there and Kent State has their game uniforms on, the referees have striped shirts on. **Paul Brown** said, 'They want a football game, you give it to them.' We were only juniors then. It was in spring. We beat them so bad they walked off the field before the fourth quarter was over. We clobbered 'em. They went on to win the conference championship that year."

**Ray Getz**

**All-Ohio, 1939, Co-Captain, 1940**

*—on Massillon's 47-0 win over Kent State.*

**"It's the best football team I've ever coached. When a team can be hit** on the chin and come back like this one did it really has something."

**Paul E. Brown**

**Massillon Quarterback, 1923-25**
**Championship Coach: Massillon Tigers, Ohio State Buckeyes and Cleveland Browns**
**Coach of 14 Championship teams**
**Founder, Head Coach, GM, Cincinnati Bengals**

*—on his 1940 Massillon team, following their 34-6 over Canton McKinley. McKinley scored first and led 6-0— the only points scored against Massillon that season.*

**"From my sixth-grade year on, every year was an exciting football** year, under **Chuck Mather** and later **Tom Harp.** There was always excitement generated for all of the football games. Just being there in Massillon, being a part of it, was exciting."

**Homer Floyd**

**Legendary Massillon running back, 1952-54, All-Ohio, 1954**
**University of Kansas Star, 1955-58**

*—on the years1948-54, when Massillon was state champions each year.*

**"We were a great football team in 1982. We were 12-1, got beat by** Cincinnati Moeller. We were outmatched. When they were getting kids from three different states and all over Cincinnati like they were it was very tough to compete against them. Any other school in the state or the nation, I believe, we would have beaten handily. We had great players, **Jimmy Bushe, Tommy Gruno, Tim Sampsel, Brian Dewitz, Jimmy Geiser, Tim Sweterlitch, Donny Elavsky, Ty Beadle, Charles Calhoun.** These guys were all tough, good, solid football players. I think that was one of Massillon's finest teams, 1982."

**Chris Spielman**

**Massillon: 2-time All-Ohioan, All-American,**
**USA Today Defensive Player of the Year, 1983**
**Ohio State: 2-time All-American,**
**Lombardi Award Winner**
**NFL: Detroit Lions, Buffalo Bills, Since 1988**
**Four Pro Bowls**

*—on the 1982 state runner-up Tigers.*

**TIGER TALES**

Under Chuck Mather (1948-53) Massillon won six state titles, losing only three games. Two of the losses were to teams coached by former Massillon players, Augie Morningstar and Mel Knowlton.

**"I don't think there was ever a team more courageous than the** 1972 team. We won 10 games and gave up four touchdowns. I think they epitomized what Massillon stands for. Because you have guys like **Tommy Balizet** in there at nose guard at 147. **Brian Bash** was the best defensive end in the league at 165 pounds. And **Mike Green**, who was deaf and had his helmet wired so he could hear, was a two way tackle at 178 pounds. Our guards, **Larry Mayles** and **Dan Guiffre** were around 150 pounds. We had some guys with legitimate size and speed, like **Tommy Hannon**, **Bobby Geiser,** the twin boys, **Terry** and **Dari Edwards** and **Kevin Westover** quarterbacking. That team wasn't supposed to be a State Championship team."

**Bob Commings**

**Massillon Championship Coach, 1969-1973**
**State Champs, 1970**
**Head Coach, University of Iowa**

*—on his1972 team that finished the regular season 10-0 and were voted State Champions in the Associated Press poll, before losing Ohio's first-ever playoff game, 17-14, to Cincinnati Princeton.*

# Obie

## THREE FORMS—ALL BELOVED

Obie is like Santa Claus in Massillon. Children are sometimes scared of him. Santa delivers presents, Obie helps Massillon win football games. The original Obie is an instrument-playing band member in a real tiger skin—and has been since 1938.

The artistic rendition of Obie is an enduring mascot, created by an unidentified artist. Two similar versions of Obie began appearing in Tyson Roller Bearings ads in Massillon football programs in 1939. Most likely someone at Tyson's created both the running Obie—most associated with Massillon football—and the less-familiar "close-up" Obie, with his helmet askew.

The "live" tiger version of Obie started prowling the Massillon sidelines in 1970. Each year a tiger cub, loaned to Massillon by a zoo, receives treatment befitting a king during its stay. Donations are collected at Massillon home games to help pay for the tiger cub's care.

**"Paul Brown and I were in Pittsburgh watching the University** of Pittsburgh play. Between halves, out came a Panther. Two fellas in uniform with three socks on and something over their head. It was the lousiest thing you'd ever seen, with all due respect to the University of Pittsburgh. Paul turned to me and laughed a little bit. We had quite a little discussion and he said, 'Why can't we have a tiger skin, L.J.? A real tiger skin.' I said, 'Why not?' They passed a resolution by the Athletic Board and in a couple of weeks we had the nicest tiger skin."

**L.J. Smith**

**Massillon Superintendent of Schools**

*—on the birth of Obie, Massillon's mascot.*

**"Everyone thinks I designed Obie. I've met three people who claim** to have designed Obie. I did not. We really don't know who did."

**Junie Studer**

**Massillon Tiger Sign Painter**

**Booster Club President, 1972**

*—on the curious origin of Massillon's beloved mascot.*

*Obie*

**"Obie candidates have to write an essay** about why they want to be Obie. Then they have to put together a three-minute routine that they do in the skin. They have to show how they're going to bring that costume to life. Obie needs big movements, they have to bring that character to life. They have to be energetic. They have to be able to prepare their own routines for the things we do each week. It has to be somebody who likes kids. Everybody kind of brings their own "take" to Obie, depending on what kind of personality they have. It's fun to watch that."

**Chris Smith**

**Massillon Band Director, Since 1991**

*—on selecting a band member to play Obie.*

**"It was dark and dingy when you came out of Mansfield's locker room.** Assistant coach **Kenny Wable** said, 'O.K. fellas, I think we're going to win this one tonight.' Then he burst out the door to go to the press box. He opened the door into the darkness and ran out—and Obie, that big Tiger, was standing there. He ran right into him. He said, 'Uh, uh, *Hi Obie.*' It was a funny situation."

**Tom Harp**

**Massillon Championship Head Coach, 1954-55**
**State Champs, 1954**
**Head Coach Duke, Cornell, Indiana State**
**Assistant to Colonel Blake at Army**

*—on his assistant coach being scared by mascot Obie.*

**"The live tiger is used for education. They go out and talk with the kids** about tigers. The kids at school study about tigers, where their habitat is—we tie that into education. The band's Tiger is for entertainment. When you see the little kids' faces—and adults' faces when Obie comes up to shake their hand...it's beautiful."

**Chris Smith**

**Massillon Band Director, Since 1991**

*—on the roles of Massillon's live and mascot Obie.*

# Today and Tomorrow

## FOREVER MASSILLON

Over a century of football excellence. Massillon is a one-of-a-kind town, in love with its football team—and all the pageantry that goes with it.

Total community involvement in the football team brings together people from all walks of life. Massillon is a town with a fierce desire to win—but not at all costs.

Good sports who just don't like to lose. People who want to be the best in everything they do. A strong determination to do what's right for the kids. Massillon people love to see their kids excel.

People who proudly say, *"I'm from Massillon."*

**"The greatest thing about Massillon is that the football is always gonna** be there. There's always going to be the enthusiasm. There's always going to be the hoopla and the great fans. The people just won't let go of that. It's steeped in tradition. It's got the greatest history in high school football. We're going to always be a contender. The ghosts of the past will make sure of that."

**Nick Vrotsos**

**Legendary Massillon Assistant, 1958-84**

*—on the future of Massillon football.*

**"Face it, Massillon expects too much. If we don't win, I don't know** how you're going to keep this community happy. It's a tough racket. I don't envy any coach coming in here. The expectations. People still think they oughta be state champions every year. And that's not gonna happen anymore. It's sort of unfair to the kids in a way, to expect them to do better than they're physically able to do."

**Jim Snively**

**Team Dentist**

**School Board President**

*—on the expectations of Massillon fans.*

*Massillon Washington High School and Tiger Stadium.*
(Photo by Gallery Studio, Massillon, Ohio)

**"Massillon was hurt badly when Republic Steel scaled down, of** course, a lot of the young people moved away. But it's rebounded rather dramatically. I sense that spirit is there. You can't miss it if you go to a football game. That high school is awesome—that's quite an amazing feat for a town that size. I feel that spirit. I think that spirit is what keeps Massillon humming."

**David Canary**

**All-Ohio, 1956**
**All-American, University of Cincinnati, 1959**
**4-Time Emmy Winner, "All My Children"**
**"Candy" on "Bonanza"**

*—on Massillon's spirit.*

**"I really think that fate has brought me here. This is my destiny.**

**Rick Shepas**

**New Massillon Head Coach**

*—on his job as Massillon's Head Coach.*

**"We've got to get the attention back on Massillon. Right now the** attention and focus is not on Massillon. It's hard for Massillon to uphold these traditions over all these years. Somewhere along the line we have to make sure we get that attention and focus back on us."

**Rick Shepas**

**New Massillon Head Coach**

*—on restoring Massillon as the leading football power.*

**Nothing in the world is supposed to last this long. Governments** and countries sometimes don't last this long. Massillon has only one losing season in 67 years. For some incredible reason, Massillon has lasted."

**Bill Oliver**

**Longtime Massillon Fan**

*—on Massillon's record of one losing season since 1931.*

**“The difference between the people of Massillon and people in other** places is that Massillon people *care* more. The legacy was started by Paul Brown and it continued. There were a few times it faltered. Never fallen—faltered. The thing my predecessor, Bob Seaman, didn’t grasp was that you’ve got to adhere to tradition. You’ve got to call on that. You don’t just send a Massillon kid out and assume that because he’s a Massillon kid he’s going to play well. You’ve got to make that kid aware of what he stands for. Aware of what he’s responsible for. Don’t take your tradition for granted. You have to work a little harder. You have to understand when you go out there every Friday night you have to play to your tradition.”

**Bob Commings**

**Massillon Championship Head Coach, 1969-73**
**State Champs, #2 in Nation, 1970**
**Head Coach, University of Iowa, 1974**

*—on the head coach’s responsibility for carrying on the Massillon tradition.*

**“In Massillon, we want to be number one and we don’t want to** apologize for it. There’s a uniqueness here, there’s a one-ness here that you just don’t want to see go down the drain. I think the forefathers in this town understood that. I just hope that the attitude never changes.”

**Bob Commings**

**Massillon Championship Head Coach, 1969-73**
**State Champs, #2 in Nation, 1970**
**Head Coach, University of Iowa, 1974**

*—on Massillon’s winning attitude.*

**“In Massillon being successful isn’t based on having a winning season. In other words, that’s not good enough. Here, if you’re 6-4 you’ve got big trouble.”**

**Junie Studer**

**Massillon Tiger Sign Painter**
**Booster Club President, 1972**

*—on Massillon’s high expectations.*

**"We just have to realize that sometimes other teams are going** to be better than Massillon. Massillon's not going to win every football game. There's going to be teams that are better. You've got to see that the team is well prepared and that they play as hard as they can. I think that's the most important thing."

**Travis McGuire**

**All-Ohio Running Back, 1991**
**Stark County Player of the Year, 1991**
**Ohio Offensive Player of the Year, 1991**

*—on the need for realistic expectations of the team.*

**"I'm coming to the end here. Because there's a life expectancy for** coaches here. I've gone beyond that life expectancy. So there's a good chance this is probably it for me. I understand that. I knew that going in. But it will probably be the highlight of my coaching career, coaching here."

**Jack Rose**

**Massillon Head Coach, 1992-97**

*—on Massillon's tradition of coaches having success then moving on.*

**"Massillon needs to get everybody participating in flag and midget** league football again. That's where it all starts. That's where my dreams started. Once you get it started there, you can keep it going—kids will want to play."

**Travis McGuire**

**All-Ohio Running Back, 1991**
**Stark County Player of the Year, 1991**
**Ohio Offensive Player of the Year, 1991**

*—on the importance of grass-roots level football.*

**"This is the best place in high school coaching that you can** possibly be. A lot of football programs try to create the kind of enthusiasm that becomes contagious. But in Massillon they live it year 'round."

**Rick Shepas**

**New Massillon Tigers Head Coach**

*—on his job as Massillon's head coach.*

# Massillon's All-Ohioans
## *1925-1998*

Massillon players have received All-Ohio recognition 177times. They are listed alphabetically. The 86 players named to the first team are in **bold** type.

**Ronnie Agnes** (1953), **Charlie Anderson** (1936), Junie Anderson (1937), **Dick "R.C." Arrington** (1943), Falando Ashcraft (1991), Eric Barnard (1978), Ty Beadle (1982), Gary "Sluggo" Bednar (1958), Chuck Beiter (1957), **Ivory Benjamin** (1957), Steve Birkish (1933), **Bill "Rabbit" Blunt** (1963), **Fred "Pokey" Blunt** (1941), Tom Boone (1953), **Kevin Bouder** (1994), **Ben Bradley** (1962), **Bruce Brenner** (1951), **Al Brown** (1948), Charlie Brown (1961), Neri Buggs (1935), **Mike Byelene** (1936), **Charles Calhoun** (1982), Dave Canary (1955), **Fred Cardinal** (1941), **Clyde Childers** (1957), **Irvin "Ace" Crable** (1949), Tim Daniels (1977), Charles Danzy (1973), Joe Demando (1941), Carl Dorsey (1977), Don Duke (1955), Bob Dunwiddie (1988), Howard Dutton (1935), **Dave Eberhart** (1980), Doug Everhart (1980), **Ron Ertle** (1967), **Homer Floyd** (1954), Will Foster (1966), **John Francisco** (1953), Dennis Franklin (1970), **Bill Gable** (1944), **Jim Geiser** (1952), Ray Getz (1939), **Horace Gillom** (1939-40), **Bob Glass** (1935-37), Anthony Grizzard (1976), Tom Grizzard (1975), Henry "Ace" Grooms (1951), Tom Gruno (1983), Marty Guzzetta (1979), **Dan Hackenbracht** (1992), **Tom Hannon** (1972), **Bill Harmon** (1975), *(Continued)*

# Massillon's All-Ohioans

*(Continued)*

**Art Hastings** (1959-60), **Rick Heather** (1981), Gene Henderson (1939), Courtney Herring (1994), **Mike Hershberger** (1956), **John Hill** (1941), Josh Hill (1997), Lance Hostetler (1986), Tom Houser (1967), **Jack Houston** (1948), **Jim Houston** (1955), **Lin Houston** (1938), **Bob Howe** (1950), Lee Hurst (1989), **Ken Ivan** (1961), Brandon Jackson (1992), **Tommy James** (1940), Tom Jasinski (1943), Craig Johnson (1983), **Elwood Kammer** (1925), Todd Kasunick (1980), **Bob Khoenle** (1952), Mark Kircher (1979), Ray Kovacsiss (1989), **Josh Kreider** (1997), **Heine Krier** (1934), Jerry Krisher (1950), **Larry Larsuel** (1963-64), **Jim Letcavits** (1953), **Trace Liggett** (1988), Eric Lightfoot (1996), **Wendell Lohr** (1934), Darren Longshore (1978), Bud Lucius (1938), Steve Luke (1970), **Paul Marks** (1965), Earl Martin (1939), **Ramier Martin** (1989), Larry Massie (1979), **Ben Mast** (1996), **Mike Mauger** (1970), **Hase McKey** (1958-59), **Milo McGuire** (1996), **Travis McGuire** (1991), John McVay (1948), Jim Mercer (1956), Pat Midgley (1969), Jim Miller (1936), Steve Miller (1991), Christian Morgan (1997), **Augie Morningstar** (1935), John Muhlbach (1964), **Jerome Myrics** (1987), George Nikitenko (1981), Lee Nussbaum (1952), **Brent Offenbecher** (1977-78), Trevor Paisley (1993), **B.J. Payne** (1993, *(Continued)*

# Massillon's All-Ohioans

*(Continued)*

Jeff Pedro (1978), Will Perry (1963), Bill Porrini (1966), **Jim Reichenbach** (1950), **Tim Ridgley** (1970), **Jim Russell** (1939-40), John Schilling (1987), **Bruce Schram** (1953), Duane Scott (1990), Dick Shine (1949), **Wes Siegenthaler** (1985), **Bob Simpson** (1979), Lonnie Simpson (1993), **George Slusser** (1939), **Jim Smith** (1968), **Cloyd Snavely** (1934), **Don Snavely** (1936-37), **Terry Snyder** (1959), **Vince Snyder** (1938), **Joe Sparma** (1959), **Willie Spencer, Sr.** (1971), **Willie Spencer, Jr.** (1994), Bruce Spicer (1984), Mike Spicer (1980), Pat Spicer (1984), **Chris Spielman** (1982-83), Curtis Strawder (1978), Larry Strobel (1961), Joe Studer (1974), Charles Swann (1973), Fred Toles (1938), **John Traylor** (1953), **Glenn Tunning** (1951), Vinnie Turner (1995), Tony Uliveto (1946), **Jerrod Vance** (1986), **Bob Vogel** (1958), **Bill Wallace** (1940), Bob Wallace (1943), **Brutus "Burt" Webb** (1945), Vernie Weisgarber (1942), Mark Wells (1994), **Lawson White** (1960), Tom Whitfield (1964), **Dave Whitfield** (1965), Julius Whitman (1947), Bob Williams (1943), Bob Williams (1954), Leaman Williamson (1957), Mike Wilson (1986), **John Woodlock** (1987), Jason Woullard (1991), **Eric Wright** (1991), Jim Young (1946), Gene Zorger (1946), Bill Zorn (1958).

# Booster Club Presidents

Arvine "Tink" Ulrich (1934), Alvin D. Wampler (1935), C.L. Albrecht (1936), W.E.N. Hemperley (1937), Karl Young (1938), I.M. Emery (1939), H. Charles Hess (1940), H.E. Shanabrook (1941), Robert E. Smith (1942), J.A. Shaidnagle, Jr. (1943), Lionel F. Ashbolt (1944), Frank A. Ceckler (1945), H.P. Croxton (1946), Ted Roth (1947), Robert K. Willison (1948), J.W. (Bill) Snyder (1949), Robert Pietzcker (1950), Ells Myers (1951), James M. Hell (1952), Emmett Graybill (1953), Paul E. Paulson (1954), Edward R. Bordner (1955), Robert Immel, DDS (1956), James Bucher (1957), Don Ahlstrom (1958), Walter Sorg, Jr. (1959), Richard Reichel (1960), John Shaidnagle III (1961), Richard Immel (1962), Tom Straughn (1963), Charles Gumpp (1964), John Reusser (1965), Richard Woolbert (1966), Jack "Bunker" Hill (1967), Duane Knight (1968), Ronald Wright (1969), Wilbur Arnold, Jr. (1970), Donald McFarren (1971), Paul "Junie" Studer (1972), Gene Boerner (1973), Jim Bryan (1974), Earl J. O'Leary (1975), John Muhlbach (1976), Dennis Gibson (1977), Pete Spuhler (1978), Tom Converse (1979), Jim Weber (1980), Al Rogers (1981), Gary Wilson (1982), Ed Annen (1983), Bob Bushman (1984), Phillip Elum (1985), John Catlin (1986), Ed Jordan (1987), Phillip C. Glick (1988), Gary Vogt (1989), Don Wilton (1990), Glen Weirich (1991), Jeff Thornberry (1992), Rollie Layfield (1993), Clarence Rambaud (1994), Bob Marks (1995), John Hauser (1996), Jeff Bushman (1997), Ron Pribich (1998).

# The Coaches

| Coach | Record |
|---|---|
| **Hap Fugate (1909-10)** | **13-4-3** |
| Sidney Jones (1912-13) | 9-9-1 |
| **John Snavely (1914-19)** | **41-8-2** |
| Elmer Snyder (1920) | 3-4-1 |
| **Dave Stewart (1921-25)** | **38-9-0** |
| Dan Atkinson (1926-27) | 8-7-3 |
| Elmer McGrew (1928-31) | 20-16-4 |
| **Paul E. Brown** (1932-40) | **80-8-2** |
| Bud Houghton (1941, 1946-47) | 21-6-3 |
| **Elwood Kammer** (1942-44) | **26-4-0** |
| Augie Morningstar (1945) | 5-0-5 |
| **Chuck Mather** (1948-53) | **57-3-0** |
| **Tom Harp** (1954-55) | **17-2-1** |
| **Lee Tressel** (1956-57) | **16-3-0** |
| **Leo Strang** (1958-63) | **54-8-1** |
| **Earle Bruce** (1964-65) | **20-0-0** |
| Bob Seaman (1966-68) | 20-9-1 |
| **Bob Commings** (1969-73) | **43-6-2** |
| Chuck Shuff (1974-75) | 12-7-1 |
| **Mike Currence** (1976-84) | **79-16-2** |
| John Moronto (1985-87) | 20-10-0 |
| Lee Owens (1988-91) | 35-13-0 |
| Jack Rose (1992-97) | 48-17-0 |

# Career Leaders

## Career Scoring Leaders

| | | | |
|---|---|---|---|
| 1 | Bob Glass | 1935-37 | 331 |
| 2 | Heine Krier | 1932-34 | 248 |
| 3 | Falando Ashcraft | 1989-91 | 244 |
| 4 | Art Hastings | 1958-60 | 240 |
| 5 | John Traylor | 1951-53 | 216 |

## Career Rushing Leaders

| | | | |
|---|---|---|---|
| 1 | Art Hastings | 1958-60 | 3,090 |
| 2 | Falando Ashcraft | 1989-91 | 2,794 |
| 3 | Travis McGuire | 1990-91 | 2,511 |
| 4 | Bill Harmon | 1973-75 | 2,505 |
| 5 | Homer Floyd | 192-54 | 2,370 |

## Career Touchdown Passes Leaders

| | | | |
|---|---|---|---|
| 1 | Mike Byelene | 1934-36 | 34 |
| 2 | Joe Sparma | 1957-59 | 31 |
| 3 | Brian Dewitz | 1982-83 | 25 |
| 4 | Mike Danzy | 1991-93 | 23 |
| 5t | Brent Offenbecher | 1976-78 | 22 |
| 5t | Lee Hurst | 1987-89 | 22 |

## Career Touchdown Catches Leaders

| | | | |
|---|---|---|---|
| 1 | Horace Gillom | 1938-40 | 18 |
| 2 | Wendell Lohr | 1933-34 | 14 |
| 3t | Rick Paige | 1964-65 | 11 |
| 3t | Larry Harper | 1969-70 | 11 |
| 4t | Gary Conley | 1981-82 | 10 |
| 4t | Alonzo Simpson | 1992-93 | 10 |

# Massillon-Canton

| No. | Year | M-C |
| --- | --- | --- |
| 1 | 1894 | 6-16 |
| 2 | 1894 | 8-12 |
| 3 | 1895 | 0-6 |
| 4 | 1900 | 0-5 |
| 5 | 1900 | 0-46 |
| 6 | 1903 | 0-5 |
| 7 | 1903 | 0-8 |
| 8 | 1904 | 0-18 |
| 9 | 1904 | 5-12 |
| 10 | 1906 | 0-24 |
| 11 | 1906 | 0-28 |
| 12 | 1907 | 0-0 |
| 13 | 1907 | 0-44 |
| 14 | 1908 | 0-17 |
| 15 | 1908 | 12-6 |
| 16 | 1909 | 11-6 |
| 17 | 1909 | 11-6 |
| 18 | 1912 | 0-19 |
| 19 | 1913 | 13-13 |
| 20 | 1914 | 3-0 |
| 21 | 1915 | 6-7 |
| 22 | 1916 | 16-9 |
| 23 | 1917 | 7-6 |
| 24 | 1919 | 21-0 |
| 25 | 1920 | 0-14 |
| 26 | 1921 | 13-12 |

| No. | Year | M-C |
| --- | --- | --- |
| 27 | 1922 | 24-0 |
| 28 | 1923 | 9-0 |
| 29 | 1924 | 6-0 |
| 30 | 1925 | 3-6 |
| 31 | 1926 | 0-0 |
| 32 | 1927 | 0-13 |
| 33 | 1928 | 0-7 |
| 34 | 1929 | 31-6 |
| 35 | 1930 | 14-6 |
| 36 | 1931 | 20-6 |
| 37 | 1932 | 0-19 |
| 38 | 1933 | 0-21 |
| 39 | 1934 | 6-21 |
| 40 | 1935 | 6-0 |
| 41 | 1936 | 21-0 |
| 42 | 1937 | 19-6 |
| 43 | 1938 | 12-0 |
| 44 | 1939 | 20-6 |
| 45 | 1940 | 34-6 |
| 46 | 1941 | 32-0 |
| 47 | 1942 | 0-35 |
| 48 | 1943 | 21-0 |
| 49 | 1944 | 0-27 |
| 50 | 1945 | 0-0 |
| 51 | 1946 | 6-6 |
| 52 | 1947 | 0-14 |

# Massillon-Canton

| No. | Year | M-C |
|---|---|---|
| 53 | 1948 | 21-12 |
| 54 | 1949 | 6-0 |
| 55 | 1950 | 33-0 |
| 56 | 1951 | 40-0 |
| 57 | 1952 | 41-8 |
| 58 | 1953 | 48-7 |
| 59 | 1954 | 26-6 |
| 60 | 1955 | 7-13 |
| 61 | 1956 | 7-34 |
| 62 | 1957 | 25-7 |
| 63 | 1958 | 38-16 |
| 64 | 1959 | 20-0 |
| 65 | 1960 | 42-0 |
| 66 | 1961 | 7-6 |
| 67 | 1963 | 24-2- |
| 68 | 1963 | 22-6 |
| 69 | 1964 | 20-14 |
| 70 | 1965 | 18-14 |
| 71 | 1966 | 16-25 |
| 72 | 1967 | 20-15 |
| 73 | 1968 | 6-26 |
| 74 | 1969 | 7-14 |
| 75 | 1970 | 28-0 |
| 76 | 1971 | 29-6 |
| 77 | 1972 | 12-3 |
| 78 | 1973 | 0-21 |

| No. | Year | M-C |
|---|---|---|
| 79 | 1974 | 20-15 |
| 80 | 1975 | 15-21 |
| 81 | 1976 | 7-3 |
| 82 | 1977 | 21-0 |
| 83 | 1978 | 13-10 |
| 84 | 1979 | 24-0 |
| 85 | 1980 | 7-16 |
| 86 | 1980 | 14-6 |
| 87 | 1981 | 15-18 |
| 88 | 1982 | 7-0 |
| 89 | 1983 | 18-7 |
| 90 | 1984 | 7-20 |
| 91 | 1985 | 6-21 |
| 92 | 1986 | 6-23 |
| 93 | 1987 | 15-18 |
| 94 | 1988 | 10-7 |
| 95 | 1989 | 24-7 |
| 96 | 1990 | 7-20 |
| 97 | 1991 | 42-13 |
| 98 | 1992 | 6-14 |
| 99 | 1993 | 13-21 |
| 100 | 1994 | 42-41 |
| 101 | 1994 | 20-27 |
| 102 | 1995 | 21-24 |
| 103 | 1996 | 0-21 |
| 104 | 1997 | 14-27 |

# Championship Teams

| Year | Record | Coach | M | Opp. |
|---|---|---|---|---|
| 1922 | 10-0-0 | Dave Stewart | 379 | 28 |
| 1935 | 10-0-0 | Paul E. Brown | 483 | 13 |
| 1936 | 10-0-0 | Paul E. Brown | 443 | 14 |
| 1937 | 8-1-1 | Paul E. Brown | 228 | 50 |
| 1938 | 10-0-0 | Paul E. Brown | 302 | 60 |
| 1939 | 10-0-0 | Paul E. Brown | 460 | 25 |
| 1940 | 10-0-0 | Paul E. Brown | 477 | 6 |
| 1941 | 9-0-1 | Bud Houghton | 314 | 37 |
| 1943 | 10-0-0 | Elwood Kammer | 278 | 12 |
| 1948 | 9-1-0 | Chuck Mather | 271 | 95 |
| 1949 | 9-1-0 | Chuck Mather | 395 | 93 |
| 1950 | 10-0-0 | Chuck Mather | 407 | 37 |
| 1951 | 9-1-0 | Chuck Mather | 316 | 65 |
| 1952 | 10-0-0 | Chuck Mather | 437 | 93 |
| 1953 | 10-0-0 | Chuck Mather | 399 | 55 |
| 1954 | 9-1-0 | Tom Harp | 295 | 66 |
| 1959 | 10-0-0 | Leo Strang | 432 | 46 |
| 1960 | 10-1-0 | Leo Strang | 348 | 93 |
| 1961 | 11-0-0 | Leo Strang | 332 | 64 |
| 1964 | 10-0-0 | Earle Bruce | 297 | 48 |
| 1965 | 10-0-0 | Earle Bruce | 247 | 78 |
| 1970 | 10-0-0 | Bob Commings | 412 | 29 |

# Attendance Records

| **All-Time Attendance** | **Over 8 million** | |
|---|---|---|
| **Largest Home Crowd** | 22,645 | 1964 |

## Largest Away Crowds:

| | | | |
|---|---|---|---|
| 1 | Cleveland Stadium | 51,000 | 1945 |
| 2 | Akron Rubber Bowl | 33,000 | 1940 |
| 3 | Akron Rubber Bowl | 32,219 | 1994 |
| 4 | Ohio Stadium | 31,409 | 1982 |
| 5 | Akron Rubber Bowl | 30,128 | 1964 |

## Top Seasons, Average Total Attendance

| Rank | Overall Attendance | Average | Year |
|---|---|---|---|
| 1 | 187,500 | 18,750 | 1945 |
| 2 | 180,500 | 18,050 | 1940 |
| 3 | 153,000 | 15,300 | 1941 |
| 4 | 152,998 | 15,299 | 1947 |
| 5 | 147,548 | 14,548 | 1967 |
| 6 | 143,507 | 14,350 | 1964 |
| 7 | 142,810 | 14,281 | 1965 |
| 8 | 141,164 | 14,116 | 1966 |
| 9 | 155,144 | 14,104 | 1972 |
| 10 | 182,658 | 14,050 | 1982 |

*The 1955 band was the first band east of the Mississippi to appear in the Tournament of Roses Parade.*

# Band Performances

Rose Bowl Parade
Peach Bowl Parade
Cotton Bowl Parade
Disneyworld
Disneyland

Gimbel's Thanksgiving Parade
Macy's Thanksgiving Parade
Cherry Blossom Parade
Saint Patrick's Day Parade
Hudson's Thanksgiving Parade

National Football League: Cleveland, Cincinnati, Buffalo, Pittsburgh, Detroit, Green Bay, All-Star game, Hall of Fame Game.
Named "Official Marching Band" of *Nick at Night's TV Land* television network.

*Paul Brown Tiger Stadium—Home of the Massillon Tigers.*
(Photo by Gallery Studio, Massillon, Ohio)

# Index

## A



## B

## C



## D

## E



## F



## G

## H

## I



## J



## K

## L



## M

## N



## O



## P

## R



## S

## T



## U



## V



## W

## Y



## Z

*Paul E. Brown, 1936*